Give Us This Day

Give Us This Day

DAILY HOPE FOR CAREGIVERS

MARTHA EVANS SPARKS

wesleyan
publishing
house

Indianapolis, Indiana

For Emily, who prays for me

Contents

How It All Started

"Cheese and crackers for dessert? You?" I exclaimed. A fine cheese makes an elegant dessert, but Bert had always preferred ice cream. I had just ordered tortoni, supposing he would follow suit.

It was Christmastime 1951, and New York City was at its glamorous best. We were finishing dinner at Luigi's, a Greenwich Village favorite. The short winter evening turned to night as we watched lower Sixth Avenue's kaleidoscope of lights and people. I was in town briefly from three states away, sharing the holidays with the man I loved most in the world, Bertel Sparks, who had asked me to marry him.

"Did my dinner order seem strange to you tonight?" he asked. We had just finished chicken cacciatore.

"No, nothing except the cheese and crackers," I replied.

"I don't eat quite like I once did. Not much change—just a little." His voice was cautious, as if he were fearful I would run away. His sudden tentativeness perplexed me.

"I have diabetes now, like Ray," he continued. Ray was his brother, who developed insulin-dependent diabetes (Type 1) when he was seventeen years old. A cousin had developed diabetes at age three. Now the family's favorite disease had struck again.

Bert had waited to tell me the bad news until we could talk face-to-face in a setting carefully selected to deliver this ominous news. He told me that he had been diagnosed the previous October and hospitalized for a week to learn how to manage the disease. Honorable man that he was, Bert would not have married me without telling me about his health problem. In fact, he urged me to talk with a doctor to find out more. I did so, although I was sure from the outset that what I heard would not halt our wedding plans. Bert seemed to be in control of the situation; how much difference could some chronic ailment make?

We married the next August, not realizing the extent to which his diabetes would shape our lives. He was thirty-four; I was nine years younger. We had met four years earlier at the University of Kentucky when I was a senior in college and he was a senior in law school. Like many in Bert's generation, his education had been delayed by World War II.

Bert was a lawyer and became a professor of law at two outstanding schools: first at New York University, later at Duke University. Over the course of a long career, he published two books and numerous articles in professional journals. On Sundays he took a busman's holiday and taught a Bible study group at our church.

I should emphasize that Bert suffered from Type 1 diabetes. This is the kind that usually affects children and young persons and accounts for about only ten percent of all cases of diabetes. All Type 1 diabetics must inject insulin in order to live. The more common form of diabetes, Type 2, typically strikes persons in middle life. No cure exists for either type.

Normal human bodies manufacture a protein called insulin. Without it, the body cannot use the energy from the food that has been consumed. A healthy body matches insulin production to food intake. Unlike native insulin, injected insulin does not stop acting when the available food is digested. If the diabetic person has eaten too little, the free insulin keeps working, pushing blood sugar too low. Insulin shock, also called insulin reaction or hypoglycemia, may result. It can produce symptoms rather like drunkenness, with irresponsible and perhaps belligerent behavior. First aid consists of feeding the person high carbohydrate food such as hard candy, sugar, or fruit juice. Left untreated, insulin reaction can result in unconsciousness and, in extreme cases, brain damage or even death.

On the other hand, if the diabetic eats too much and not enough insulin is available to cope with it, blood sugar goes too high. If this happens often, over time complications will almost certainly appear. Blindness and kidney failure are common difficulties, as is diabetic neuropathy, which produces numbness and sores that will not heal, usually beginning in the feet. Sometimes amputation of toes, feet, or even legs becomes necessary. Sustained high blood sugar levels can be life threatening.

I did not manage Bert's diabetes. He did. Bert understood that keeping his blood sugar as close as possible to normal would minimize the risk of encountering other health problems. The tight control paid handsome dividends. Bert taught and carried a full workload until he was seventy years old. Thousands of law students and more than forty years of mostly good health later, he died of pneumonia without having developed the major complications so common to his disease.

Through the years we praised the Lord for His mercy, knowing that we were working together with Him to maintain Bert's health through Bert's rigorous self-control and my support.

Throughout our marriage, diabetes management colored every part of our lives. These meditations grow out of the triumphs, catastrophes, social maneuverings, and days of small things that living with this dreadful disease forced upon us.

For the first thirty-five years or so of our nearly forty-two year marriage, I did not think of myself as a caregiver. Bert made the decisions on insulin doses and injected them himself. He planned how much and when he needed to eat. He was a busy teacher and lawyer with heavy professional responsibilities, but he always came home to lunch. My role revolved around providing three meals a day from carefully planned menus, the right food ready at the same time each day. I made certain, tactfully I hope, that we did not issue or accept any invitations that interfered greatly with his diabetic regimen. He was usually able to manage the occasional bout of low blood sugar. It is almost impossible to avoid insulin reactions entirely when the diabetic is exercising "tight control," that is, working hard to keep blood sugars in the normal range.

After his retirement, in the last six years of Bert's life, his mental status gradually changed, and my caregiving role became much more demanding. He could be left alone only for short periods. He could not deal with his diabetes. Bert referred all family financial decisions to me. Personal care became difficult for him to manage alone. His doctors ascribed his problems to little strokes, but this proved to be untrue. An autopsy disclosed extensive amyloid deposits in his brain that had caused most of the mental deterioration. Amyloid is an abnormal protein that infiltrates healthy tissue with waxy, nonfunctioning material. What caused it in Bert's case is unknown. That it had any relationship to the diabetes is uncertain. He also may have had undiagnosed Parkinson's disease.

In addition to maintaining the meal schedule and detailed menu planning, in those last years I developed expertise in caregiving tasks. These ranged from routine things like taking blood pressure, giving the insulin injections, and doing the blood sugar tests, to more demanding tasks like coping with insulin reactions in the middle of the night—a terrifying situation when the patient is bigger and stronger than the caregiver.

Caregivers for chronically ill persons have much in common, no matter what the illness.

While some experiences described in these meditations are peculiar to diabetes, most of the lessons apply to any implacable medical situation. Physically confined and isolated, caregivers cannot leave home without arranging for the sick person's care. Caregiving is mentally and emotionally draining because the caregiver must watch the loved one struggle endlessly.

Ideally, those closest to the victim of a chronic medical condition—usually his or her family members—form an emotional and medical support group for the patient. But who supports the caregiver?

That is what these meditations are about. They are intended as spiritual food for the caregiver herself or himself.

After my husband's death, I found among his papers more than one thousand short prayers, each neatly typed on a separate three-by-five card. They reflect the anguish and victory of the Christian whose thorn in the flesh the Lord chooses not to take away. Most of the prayers at the close of the meditations are Bert's. The meditations and a few of the prayers are mine.

MARTHA EVANS SPARKS

Acknowledgements

I should like to thank my old friends Donald and Eleanor Harle, who, after reading some of my husband's prayers, encouraged me to pursue the writing of this book. Through them I met the late Barbara Dean Barnes, M.D., neurologist and nature photographer, who also encouraged publication. My sincere gratitude goes to Lawrence W. Wilson, managing editor of Wesleyan Publishing House, for his excellent editorial judgment, practical help, and cheerful patience in bringing this project to completion.

Self-Worth

Esteem

Hear, O LORD, and answer me, for I am poor and needy. . . . Bring joy to your servant, for to you, O Lord, I lift up my soul.

—Psalm 86:1, 4

Point of Hope

What I am doing today is important to God.

Increased medical knowledge is bringing longer life spans but not always perfect health. As a result, many caregivers, usually women, spend much of their time looking after incapacitated family members—aging parents, a spouse with Alzheimer's, or perhaps a child with a chronic illness. No matter what the ailment, caregiving is physically, mentally, and emotionally exhausting. I know because I did it for many years.

As a young adult, my husband, Bert, developed Type 1 diabetes. He had a normal life span and a productive career, managing the disease successfully for more than forty years. From the first day of our marriage, keeping Bert healthy was a team effort. That effort began with God, whose mercy spared Bert the catastrophic complications of diabetes. Next came Bert's superb self-discipline. He never broke diabetic exercise and diet rules.

And there I was, staying at home to coordinate it all. Sometimes I thought myself insignificant. At such times, how comforting it was to cry to God the words of today's scripture, "Hear, O LORD," knowing that He heard, loved, and understood.

Point of Help

I will remember that I am important to God; even the hairs of my head are numbered (Matt. 10:30).

Bert's Prayer

We go to church and listen to the gospel. We know the words, but we have not made them a part of our being. Our Lord and our God, let the truth break upon me afresh, as if it had been concealed up to now. Let me experience the joy that comes to one who, for the first time, learns that somebody cares. Teach me to care.

Confidence

But Moses said to God, "Who am I, that I should go to Pharaoh and bring the Israelites out of Egypt?" And God said, "I will be with you."

—Exodus 3:11–12

Point of Hope

God's children know to whose family they belong and are proud of it.

God does not desert His redeemed child to the identity-crisis quagmire. In fact, the entire Bible is an elaboration of God's answer to our "Who am I?" questions.

"Who am I?" said Adam and Eve. God had to reply that they were sinners (Genesis 3:16–19). But He promised to rescue them from the evil they had embraced (Genesis 3:15b).

"Who am I?" asked Moses, and God replied, "I will be with you" (Joshua 1:5). "Who am I?" pondered Mary, and the angel responded, "Do not be afraid, Mary, you have found favor with God" (Luke 1:30). "Who am I?" inquired Paul. God's answer rings across the centuries, "You are my ambassador in chains" (Ephesians 6:20).

Caregivers working one-on-one may think that our sphere of influence is so small that we cannot be useful as anything, much less as God's ambassadors. I used to think that I was wearing my life away to no purpose as a caregiver. Finally, it dawned on me that God is not impressed with size. God looks for faithfulness in the task assigned.

The psalmist began with an embittered soul. Then he discovered that God was always with him, holding his right hand (Ps. 73:21–23). I must have worth if God bothers to hold my hand. "You guide me with your counsel," he says to God, "and afterward you will take me into glory" (Ps. 73:24).

Point of Help

I will give thanks for my identity as a servant of the Lord.

Bert's Prayer

Dear Heavenly Father, this is the day the Lord has made. I shall rejoice and be glad in it. On some days it is hard to find a good reason for rejoicing, but rejoice I will. You created this day, and You have never done a vain thing. Let there be something I can do to make it an even better day.

Assistance

"My grace is sufficient for you, for my power is made perfect in weakness."

—2 Corinthians 12:9

Point of Hope

Caregivers are never the stars of the show, but their support is priceless.

In her classic book, *The Christian's Secret of a Happy Life,* Hannah Whitall Smith tells of visiting an institution for crippled children. Attendants were teaching the children to exercise in time to music. Most of them had little muscle control; they produced a random, awkward performance.

Yet one little girl, Mrs. Smith noticed, performed the exercises perfectly. This child was so severely handicapped that she could do nothing by herself. An instructor stood behind her, moving her arms in exactly the right pattern and in time to the music.

Is the lesson too simplistic to need explanation? Even Jesus said He did nothing on His own, but He acted or spoke only as the Father instructed Him (John 5:30; 8:28). Perhaps the cliché "Let go and let God" is true after all.

Paul was telling the Corinthians about his thorn in the flesh when he said that God's power was perfectly shown in Paul's weakness. Once, faced with a physical restriction of my own, I asked Bert how to cope with it emotionally. His two-word answer still rings in my mind: "Calm acceptance." Paul would have agreed. "I will boast . . . gladly about my weaknesses, so that Christ's power may rest on me," he said (2 Cor. 12:9). The mark of Bert's faith was his calm acceptance of the demands diabetes made upon him every day. How could I do less than my best to help him?

Point of Help

Although I cannot fully understand my loved one's physical hardships, I will do all I can to assist.

Bert's Prayer

Loving Lord, may I never look upon myself with contempt, for to do so is to look with contempt upon the handiwork of God. You have created me for a purpose, and, whatever my weakness, I am equal to the achievement of that end. Give me vision to see my appointed task and sense enough to perform it.

Self-Effacement

The share of the man who stayed with the supplies is to be the same as that of him who went down to the battle. All will share alike.

—1 Samuel 30:24

Point of Hope

Caregiving is a hidden ministry, but one that is known to God.

David and six hundred of his men went out to recapture their wives and property, stolen by the enemy while David and his army were away. On their way to do battle, two hundred of David's men became too exhausted to continue. They were left to watch over the baggage while the other four hundred found the enemy and won back their wives and property.

Some of the four hundred said it was not fair for the two hundred who stayed behind to share in the spoils of victory. David disagreed. He declared that both tasks were equally important; all would share alike.

My husband always went to bat for me when someone asked what my career was. "She takes care of me," he would say smilingly. How I loved him for it. The person who asked usually did not realize how literally true that was. Without me to have meals of the proper kind ready at the right time, three times a day, nearly 365 days a year, it would not have been possible for Bert to be so productive in his profession.

Let us never fall victim to Satan's whisper that because we are "just caregivers" our lives do not amount to anything. David reflected God's attitude, I think, when he said that those who stayed with the supplies were worthy of the same reward as those who went into battle. After all, the victory was God's, not theirs (1 Sam. 30:23).

Point of Help

I will do what I can to make my loved one's life as normal as possible because I know that God deems my labor important.

Bert's Prayer

Dear heavenly Father, whether the tasks assigned to me are large or small is not important. The question is, how do I perform them? Give me a spirit of gratitude that I may be thankful for the task, whatever it is, and that I may do what I have been called upon to do. Give me a clean heart and a willingness to serve.

Refocusing

I keep asking that the God of our Lord Jesus Christ, the glorious Father, may give you the Spirit of wisdom and revelation, so that you may know . . . the hope to which he has called you.

−Ephesians 1:17–18

Point of Hope

When we are sorry for ourselves, God gives us not sympathy but a new outlook.

Caregivers for the chronically ill are prone to a condition called the Why-Me-Lord Blues. When people in the Bible felt this brand of self-pity, the Lord gave them a new revelation of Himself and sent them back to work.

Elijah fled from Queen Jezebel in utter discouragement. Elijah concluded that he was the only true worshiper of Jehovah left (1 Kings 19:10). God demonstrated His power to the prophet in ways Elijah never forgot. After wind, earthquake, and fire, God's presence came in "a gentle whisper." Then God gave Elijah specific tasks: the anointing of two new kings and a new prophet (1 Kings 19:11–16).

Four days after Lazarus died, his sister Martha looked straight into the face of God and said it was hopeless. Jesus looked right back, and His words gave her a new idea of what constitutes victory in daily life. "I am the resurrection and the life," He said (John 11:25). She was given a task: believe.

The disciples, cowering behind closed doors one Sunday evening, thought Jesus was a ghost when He suddenly appeared. They soon had new work to do. "You are witnesses of these things," Jesus said and sent them to preach His gospel all over the world (Luke 24:36–49).

Point of Help

I will replenish my strength today by seeking a fresh vision of God.

Bert's Prayer

Dear Heavenly Father, it is right that we should search for wisdom, but too often we have searched in the wrong places. The only source of wisdom is in You, Eternal God. Let our search begin with praise and thanks to You. O God, as we claim Your promises, made to us, let us do so with lives that are committed to Your will.

Self-Respect

Those who grieve . . . will be called oaks of righteousness,
a planting of the LORD for the display of his splendor.
—Isaiah 61:3

Point of Hope

No work is more important than that of demonstrating what God can do in my life.

Jesus confirmed His claim to be Messiah by reading the first part of Isaiah, chapter 61, to worshipers at the synagogue in His hometown of Nazareth. It was His job description. He was "to preach good news to the poor . . . proclaim freedom for the prisoners and recovery of sight for the blind, to release the oppressed, to proclaim the year of the Lord's favor" (Luke 4:18–19).

That sounds good, but how could Jesus' job description possibly apply to me as a caregiver? I cannot go out of the house without complicated preparations. I have no personal freedom. I mourn when I remember the person my loved one was before illness struck. I can't see beyond the day's first hurdle. What freedom? What gladness?

The passage does not say you will become rich, beautiful, and free from care if you follow the Lord. It does mention a specific calling: to be an oak "of righteousness, a planting of the LORD." The reason I am to grow into that oak is not to show how strong I am, fluttering my foliage with a painted-on smile. It is "for the display of his splendor" (Isa. 61:3b).

When I'm feeling like a mowed-over sapling (as most caregivers do from time to time), I need to remember that Jesus believes I have the potential for growing into a mighty oak, worthy to display His splendor. That's why He planted me here.

Point of Help

I will thank God that my true worth is based on what He thinks of me, not what I think of myself.

Bert's Prayer

The more difficult the task, my Lord and my God, the greater is the opportunity it brings. I pray not for an easier life but for increased adequacy for the circumstances with which I am now surrounded. May I not rejoice at the failures of others, but give me the strength and the wisdom to rise above the obstacles that are left in the way.

Comfort

Power

When he saw the crowds, he had compassion on them, because they were harassed and helpless, like sheep without a shepherd.

—Matthew 9:36

Point of Hope

God "is able to do immeasurably more than all we ask or imagine" (Eph. 3:20).

Bert wrote the following.
Jesus healed:

The Leper. "A man with leprosy came and knelt before him and said, 'Lord, if you are willing, you can make me clean.'

"Jesus reached out his hand and touched the man. 'I am willing,' he said. 'Be clean!' Immediately he was cured of his leprosy" (Matt. 8:2–3).

Those with Fever. "When Jesus came into Peter's house, he saw Peter's mother-in-law lying in bed with a fever. He touched her hand and the fever left her, and she got up and began to wait on him" (Matt. 8:14–15).

The Blind. "Two blind men followed him, calling out, 'Have mercy on us, Son of David!'" . . .

The blind men came to him, and he asked them, 'Do you believe that I am able to do this?'

"'Yes, Lord,' they replied.

"Then he touched their eyes and said, 'According to your faith will it be done to you'; and their sight was restored" (Matt. 9:27–30).

Everyone. "Great crowds came to him, bringing the lame, the blind, the crippled, the mute and many others, and laid them at his feet; and he healed them" (Matt. 15:30).

Can Jesus cure diabetes? Even mine? Of course He can. But for reasons I do not understand, He does not. Remember Mary and Martha, the sisters of Lazarus, who asked for his healing and did not get it (John 11:3, 21)?

They received a resurrection instead (John 11:44).

Point of Help

I will believe that God can still do great things.

Bert's Prayer

More than nineteen centuries have passed since Jesus graced the earth. We spend so much time explaining the event that we have almost forgotten it. Forgive us, Lord, for our efforts to reduce that life to our own understanding, and restore to us a touch of its infinite power.

Compassion

Then I saw a new heaven and a new earth. . . . There will be no more death or mourning or crying or pain. . . . He who was seated on the throne said, "I am making everything new!"

—Revelation 21:1, 4–5

Point of Hope

Lord of lords and King of kings, Christ will reign forever.

I watched day after day as Bert trudged endlessly through our house between his office and the kitchen. Once so energetic and efficient, now he was fragile, ceaselessly occupied with the demands of an inflexible medical schedule. Besides the pain of injections, his fingertips stayed sore from constant blood tests. Often weary, he suffered frequent headaches. Was there ever a time when he felt good?

Dear Jesus, will it always be so?

The Spirit's hushed voice echoed gently inside my head. "No, because I make all things new."

Someday Bert would stand before the Lord in

his glorified body, and the pain would be gone. It was clear then that the Lord's will was not to heal Bert in this life. But the one who sits on the throne and declares that He makes all things new is the same person who said, "Come to me, all you who are weary and burdened, and I will give you rest" (Matt. 11:28). At that moment I realized that Bert rested his soul in the Lord now, and someday his body would rest also. Indeed, O death, where is your victory (1 Cor. 15:55)?

Point of Help

I will hold firm in the hope of the Resurrection.

Bert's Prayer

Dear Heavenly Father, it is hard to grow old. It hurts to see strength fading away. There are times when I stumble and almost lose my grip. But always You are the one who has a grip on me. As I use what strength is left, I will give thanks for the coming dawn when all things shall be made new.

Constancy

My flesh and my heart may fail, but God is the strength of my heart and my portion forever.

—Psalm 73:26

Point of Hope

Jesus Christ is the one constant in the universe.

I cried to the Lord for a healing touch for Bert. With a sore heart I turned to God's Word for comfort. Instead of the green pastures of the Twenty-third Psalm or the unbridled praise of the One Hundred Fiftieth, the Lord turned my attention to the Seventy-third Psalm.

There, the writer vacillates, it seemed to me. God is good to the upright, the psalmist says, but his own steps are about to slip because he envies the arrogant. Such people have no troubles, he thinks. They take their ease and get rich and richer. Finally, the writer realizes that it is the arrogant who are in danger of falling. In the end they will be swept away.

In spite of this insight, our song writer sees himself as stupid and ignorant (v. 22). But he clings to God, saying, "Whom have I in heaven but you?" (v. 25). Then in the next breath (v. 26), everything crashes as he laments that both his body and his spirit fail. What can be left?

What are You saying to me, Lord? Through the mistakes, through the days when there is no good solution to the problems, am I to cling to the one constant in the universe—You? "Jesus only is my cry; Jesus only or I die," says the old gospel song. Is it to you that I am to turn?

Point of Help

I'll stay on the job and give God an opportunity to show me how faithful He is.

Bert's Prayer

Lord, forbid that I should ever be satisfied because I have found a way that seems right. Various ways often spring from noble effort and seem worthy of acceptance, but their end is destruction. I cannot rest except in the Way. There will I stand, even when I appear to stand alone. There serenity reigns and promises are sure.

Presence

In my alarm I said, "I am cut off from your sight!" Yet you heard my cry for mercy when I called to you for help.
—Psalm 31:22

Point of Hope

God promises never to leave you or forsake you (Heb. 13:5).

I am alone. Every caregiver believes it sometimes. You whisper it to yourself when you think, *What if I had a heart attack, got killed in a car wreck?* It is the fear that drives an anxious imagination. *Who would know how to keep him alive, much less love him? Is anybody there?* The cry reverberates in an empty room somewhere in every caregiver's soul. *Nobody is there. Nobody cares. I am isolated and trapped.*

If you believe yourself alone, you have plenty of company, so to speak. Moses was by himself on "the far side of the desert" (Exod. 3:1)–how much further from home can you be? Paul says he had to defend himself alone before a hostile court. The prophet Jeremiah's enemies threw him into an empty cistern, abandoning him to die.

But there is more to each of these stories. Moses thought himself alone in the desert, but the angel of the Lord joined him (Exod. 3:2). Paul's friends deserted him at trial, but he reports, "the Lord stood at my side and gave me strength" (2 Tim. 4:16–17). He had God's power for company. An Ethiopian eunuch heard about Jeremiah's plight and rescued him (Jer. 38:6–13). God prompted an improbable person to meet a need.

God provided His presence, His power, His prompting. We are His children in another time and place. But God is the same. Does He love us any less or have any less power now than He did when Moses, Paul, and Jeremiah called upon Him?

Point of Help

I will take heart because I know that God will not leave me alone.

Bert's Prayer

Dear Heavenly Father, we trust You in times of plenty. Surely we can trust You in times of distress. And now as the way seems dark, may our trust be even greater. Show us where we have failed, and help us to realize that the failure is our own. Salvation is with You, and You alone.

Assurance

Surely goodness and love will follow me all the days of my life.

—Psalm 23:6

Point of Hope

I need Someone, not something.

The Bible is filled with promises of help. Why don't any of them work?

Every caregiver asks that desperate question at some time. Exhausted and frustrated, we try to trust Christ's assurance, but nothing seems to change. We aren't angry; we're exhausted. We have given to others until we are emotionally spent.

Could it be that we are looking for some thing—relief—when we should be looking for Someone—the Lord and His refreshing presence?

"The LORD your God is with you . . . he will quiet you with his love," says the prophet (Zeph. 3:17). Zephaniah directed the people toward the person of God.

"Who is this coming up from the desert leaning on her lover?" (Song of Songs 8:5). The bride, of course, arm in arm with her beloved enjoying a quiet time together.

Jehovah assured Moses, "My Presence will go with you, and I will give you rest" (Exod. 33:14). Moses famously replied, "If you won't go with us, let's not even start the trip" (Exod. 33:15, paraphrase).

Notice that in these scriptures God does not do anything. He is simply there. Haven't you known human comfort of that kind? In the presence of someone you loved and trusted, you felt at peace. He or she did not have to do anything. Presence was enough. That is the kind of deep rest the Lord wants us to find in His love. "This is what the Sovereign LORD, the Holy One of Israel, says: ' . . . in quietness and trust is your strength'" (Isa. 30:15).

Point of Help

Today I will let God's quietness fill my soul.

Bert's Prayer

Loving Lord, as I come into the presence of the Almighty, let me have both a sense of awe and an awareness of being with a Friend. In a mysterious way, You are both to me— awesome Lord and comfortable friend. For both I give thanks. Without either I am undone. Forgive my waywardness, and let me stand boldly before your presence.

Example

But we see Jesus . . . crowned with glory and honor because he suffered death, so that by the grace of God he might taste death for everyone.

—Hebrews 2:9

Point of Hope

Jesus shows us what to do when life isn't fun anymore.

The Gospels record seven things Jesus said while he hung on the Cross, often referred to as the seven last words. Can we learn anything from the way in which He faced His life's worst day?

He reached out to others. Even in agony, He remembered His mother and gave her into John's care (John 19:26–27).

He freely forgave all who had caused His desolation. "Father, forgive them," He asked. Then He added the ultimate charity: "They do not know what they are doing" (Luke 23:34).

He gave an incredible gift, eternal life, to the thief on the cross next to Him (Luke 23:43).

He understated the physical torture, but faced

it candidly. "I am thirsty," He said (John 19:28).

He was straightforward with the Father. "My God, my God, why have you forsaken me?" (Mark 15:34). It was unvarnished communication.

He committed himself utterly to God. "Father, into your hands I commit my spirit" (Luke 23:46).

He fully accepted God's will. "It is finished," Jesus said (John 19:30).

One of these reactions is beyond our power. We cannot promise anyone a place in heaven. The other six are within the scope of human possibility, aided by God. Jesus faced an awful situation simply, with the realization that God's power would be sufficient. Is there something useful here for us caregivers?

Point of Help

With God's help, today I will identify one source of stress and begin to deal with it.

Bert's Prayer

Dear Heavenly Father, it is strange that our glory should be in a cross. Give me a better understanding of that truth. Let me be used to carry that good news to others, and let my life be so faithful to the heavenly vision that my very being will be a message worthy of acceptance.

Encouragement

Confidence

She gave this name to the LORD who spoke to her: "You are the God who sees me."

—Genesis 16:13

Point of Hope

God knows where I am.

Hagar had no choice. She was a slave. Her mistress, Sarai, said, "Sleep with my husband, Abram. I'll get a child from him by you." It was not an unusual plan in Middle Eastern culture those thousands of years ago.

Hagar's resulting pregnancy put her one up on her mistress. Things got so tense between them that Hagar ran away, heading home to Egypt. The angel of the Lord, perhaps the preincarnate Christ, found her by a spring of water in the wilderness. This person seemed to know all about her. He told her the baby she carried would be a boy and that he would have a life filled with conflict. "You are El-roi," Hagar said to the man, "the God Who Sees."

Most of us did not ask for the job of caring for a chronically ill or disabled loved one. We were not prepared to face medical emergencies and were even less ready to deal with tedious days, loss of personal freedom, feelings of guilt and anger. Worse yet is the anonymity. Does anyone know? Does anyone care?

We may find it difficult to identify with the kings and prophets who march across the pages of the Bible. But here is Hagar, a helpless person facing assignment she had never sought. Like her, will we recognize El-roi, the God Who Sees, when we meet Him?

Point of Help

I will draw strength from the God who sees me and stands near me in my wilderness.

Bert's Prayer

Our Lord and our God, we know that a state of eternal joy has been provided for us, but we also know that we need not wait for it. We know even that if we do wait for it, it will never come. The invitation is here and now. The door is set before us, and it is wide open. Give us the resolve to enter.

Timeliness

When you pass through deep waters, I will be with you;
your troubles will not overwhelm you.

—Isaiah 43:2 TEV

Point of Hope

God's help is appropriate and always on time,
neither early nor late.

Corrie ten Boom tells of being swamped by a bitter
experience. She wondered how the Lord could
help her.[1] Her father asked, "When you ride into
Amsterdam, when do you buy your train ticket?"

"Why, just before I get on the train," Corrie
replied.

"That is the way the Lord does it," her father
said. "He gives you the necessary strength just
when you need it."

One day I thought Bert was taking a nap.
Instead, I found him lying on the floor, rigid, unresponsive, eyes staring into space. This was severe
insulin reaction. Unconsciousness had overcome
him before he could call for help. It was the kind
of situation that can result in brain damage. He
needed food quickly; every second counted. But I

could not feed him when he was out cold.

We kept glucagon in the house, an injectable substance that forces the liver to release its stored sugar. It must be prepared just before use. I got it ready as quickly as possible and gave Bert the injection. Then I called 911. The ambulance crew continued treatment, and in a few minutes, Bert regained consciousness with no apparent aftereffects.

Later, I realized that during the experience, I had felt neither fear nor anxiety. My hands did not shake. I did not draw a mental blank. The Lord had given me adequate help just when I needed it.

Point of Help

I will abstain from worry, knowing that the everlasting arms will be there when I need them.

Bert's Prayer

Our loving Father, knowing that we have in our hands the Word that will endure forever, and knowing that we serve Him who is able to preserve us against every adversary, how can we be afraid? Give us the joy of unlimited confidence, for we serve the One who casts out all fear.

[1]Paraphrased from Corrie ten Boom with John and Elizabeth Sherrill, *The Hiding Place* (Carmel, N.Y.: Guideposts Associates, Inc., 1971), 33.

Opportunity

They saw the works of the LORD, his wonderful deeds in the deep. . . . Let them give thanks to the LORD for his unfailing love and his wonderful deeds for men.
—Psalm 107:24, 31

Point of Help

The Lord already has a plan in place for weathering this storm.

N otice the progression of events in the tempest that the writer describes in the One Hundred Seventh Psalm. In verse twenty-three, people are going about their daily work. The Lord raises a stormy wind in verse twenty-five, an action we do not understand. By verse twenty-seven, the sailors have come to the end of their own efforts, and in verse twenty-eight, they call on the Lord for help. God stills the storm in verse twenty-nine. The writer masterfully understates the human reaction to that in verse thirty, "They were glad when it grew calm." We leave this little band thanking and praising the Lord.

Luke's story (Luke 8:22–25) parallels exactly

the events outlined in this psalm. The disciples and Jesus are crossing Lake Galilee on a justifiable errand. A gale blows up. The disciples shout at Jesus, who wakes up and stills the tempest. They worship Him in amazement.

Could it be that the emotional, financial, and medical hurricanes of our lives are merely opportunities to watch God work? In both of these cases, the people worked hard in their own strength before turning to the Lord. What would have happened if they had trusted Him earlier? Nowhere does it say that the experience was pleasant or easy, or that better management could have avoided the problems. Yet from both storms, the weather-beaten faithful emerged with an enlarged vision of God.

Point of Help

I will use the current crisis to learn something new about God's power.

Bert's Prayer

It is not easy to be grateful for pain, suffering, and disappointment. It is not easy to wear a smile when all the eye beholds seems to be falling apart. Loving Lord, give me strength for this time of testing, strength to remain calm in the midst of the storm. Let me emerge a stronger character, prepared for greater service.

Communication

What other nation is so great as to have their gods near them the way the LORD our God is near us whenever we pray to him?

—Deuteronomy 4:7

Point of Hope

Our God dwells near His people.

"The shortest distance between a problem and a solution is the distance between your knees and the floor. The person who kneels to God can stand up to anything." I do not know who said that, but when I first heard it, I took it for a shop-worn cliché. In reality, it expresses the same mighty truth Moses pointed out to Israel.

Those of us who care for the chronically ill operate sometimes in the desperation zone. It is vastly comforting to realize that our eternal God, unlike the gods of human origin who have come and gone through the centuries, is alive, well, and living nearby. He has even sent His Holy Spirit to live inside us.

We must be sure that the communication lines

between us and our nearby God are in constant use, because the miracle He works may not be the continuation of life but healing from fear or anxiety or depression— yours or your loved one's. And all of us need healing from the oppression of sin. These healings may come even as physical life slips away.

Never assume there is nothing you can do about a sick person's pain. Make sure your doctor understands how much pain is present and prescribes what he or she can to ease it. But don't retreat from it mentally, pretending it does not exist, or, at the other extreme, despairing because of it. The Nearby God is there to help you.

Point of Help

I pray that the one I care for and I will both sense the presence of God today.

Bert's Prayer

Distress comes, but it cannot conquer. God, forbid that I should try to close my eyes to the abundance of suffering, but let me not be controlled by it. When immediate wants go unsatisfied, give me patience to wait. Even when I can see no reason for the things that are, I will trust your power to perform your purpose.

Weapons

Teach me your way, O LORD. . . . For great is your love toward me; you have delivered my soul from the depths of the grave.

—Psalm 86:11, 13

Point of Hope

Caregivers can learn winning strategies.

Am I going to let this chronic disease, this medical disaster with which I must deal, overwhelm me? Can I fight against it? Can I win? What armaments do I have?

The first weapon is knowledge of God. Jesus said, "Take my yoke upon you and learn from me, for I am gentle and humble in heart, and you will find rest for your souls" (Matt. 11:29). Patient, daily Bible study and prayer provide an inner strength for days of caregiving that cannot be gotten anywhere else.

The second powerful weapon is knowledge of the disease or condition with which you must deal. Understanding your enemy gives you control. Question your doctor and pharmacist.

Inquire at the local library. Gather medical information from the Internet. The more accurate and authoritative information you have, the better off you and the person for whom you care will be.

Third, maintain friendships and keep a balanced perspective on life. I made arrangements for someone to stay with Bert for a few hours at least once a week so I could attend classes or meetings. Do not wait until you are exhausted before you find ways to get breathing space.

Yet the real victory remains a spiritual one. The prophet Jeremiah suffered much. After he endured one dark night of the soul, he emerged triumphant, observing that "the LORD is with me like a mighty warrior" (Jer. 20:11).

Point of Help

When discouragement and monotony knock, I will ask my Mighty Warrior to answer the door.

Bert's Prayer

Dear Lord, give me vision to see the open door before me. It is an invitation to the assumption of responsibility. Give me wisdom to grasp that responsibility efficiently and to carry it without fear. I will accept the assignment; the circumstances are yours.

Knowledge

There are different kinds of service, . . . but the same God works all of them in all men. Now to each one the manifestation of the Spirit is given for the common good.

—1 Corinthians 12:5–7

Point of Hope

Caregiving can be a positive learning experience.

Martin's wife, Betty, has Alzheimer's disease. Martin, a retired engineer, devotes full time to her care. I complimented him one day on how lovely Betty's hair always looks. "You must make a big effort to get her to the beauty shop," I said.

"Well," said Martin, "I was sitting in the beauty parlor one day watching the operator cut and set Betty's hair when I said to myself, 'I can do that.'" He watched the professional stylist carefully. He read and followed the directions that came with the hair color. He was right; he can do it. "It saves a lot of money," Martin says modestly.

I do not think saving money is the greatest

benefit Martin garners from taking care of Betty's hair. As the writer of Proverbs points out, "knowledge will be pleasant to your soul" (Proverbs 2:10). After hearing Martin's story, I realized that the knowledge I acquired in caregiving, while not expertise I had planned to acquire, has enabled me to help others in many ways.

The ability and opportunity to learn new things is God's gift to us. Do you remember Bezalel to whom God gave the ability "to make artistic designs for work in gold, silver and bronze" (Exod. 31:1–5)? That was God's gift, as truly as God blessed Moses with a newfound ability to speak. Who is to say that one gift was greater than the other?

Point of Help

I will view what I must learn as a caregiver as an opportunity to enrich my life.

Bert's Prayer

God, You have a work intended for me. The Eternal has assigned it to me. Forgive me, my Lord, for seeking other work. Forgive my complaints and petitions about things I am unable to do. What God has assigned, He will provide the strength for doing. If I but do that, my labor will be sufficient.

Gratitude

Service

In Christ we who are many form one body, and each member belongs to all the others.

—Romans 12:5

Point of Hope

We really do need each other.

"It was the body of Christ in action. Those people came into my house and helped me. You cannot buy love like that."

My neighbor, Lib, was referring to the last desperate days of her husband's terminal illness. The doctors had sent him home from the hospital to die in familiar surroundings. In spite of kind professional help, Lib was exhausted physically and emotionally. Then they came. Members of her church—the body of Christ, she called them—with food, hugs, tears, and loving words. They ran errands; they cleaned the house. They organized shifts, slipping quietly in and out of her husband's room. He wanted them there. He said it gave him an opportunity to say "Good-bye. I'll see you in heaven."

Those church members gave Lib comforting help. They gave more. They were not only serving her but also offering their thanks to God. "How can I repay the LORD for all his goodness to me?" cried the psalmist (Psalm 116:12). His answer was the gift of his life in praise and service to God. Paul made a similar point when he reminded us that we are one body in Christ, with many gifts to be used for God's glory. "Love must be sincere," Paul adds. "Share with God's people who are in need" (Rom. 12:5–13).

We really do need each other.

Point of Help

In return for Christ's gift of His life to me, I will give gifts of love and service to others.

Bert's Prayer

My Lord and my God, to be untrue to the heavenly vision is to be untrue to my own birthright. Help me to remember who I am and what I was meant to be. Give me grace to respond to the call of Him to whom I belong. Let my complaining cease, and let me stand with confidence before my Creator, ready for His service.

Strength

The anxious heart will understand and know.
                                    —Isaiah 32:4 NEB

Point of Hope

The more I know about God, the bigger and more adequate He becomes.

Bert woke me at 2:00 A.M., beating on the wall by his bed and calling my name. I went to him and stayed until he was quiet and reassured and I was certain he did not need anything. He drifted back to sleep.

I went back to bed wondering who was going to reassure me. I began to ponder the words of Isaiah. I wondered what that prophet's anxious heart must have known that might be relevant for me in the middle of the night, alone in the house with a semi-rational person.

When Isaiah finally got his vision of God (6:1–4), it was followed by a confession of sin (6:5) and a personal experience of God's forgiveness (6:7). From that point, the more Isaiah wrote, the bigger his God got. The prophet's familiar words tumbled through my head as I lay there in the dark.

"Do you not know? Have you not heard? The LORD . . . gives strength to the weary and increases the power of the weak" (40:28–29). "So do not fear, for I am with you; do not be dismayed, for I am your God" (41:10). And what I needed most of all that night: "I will turn the darkness into light before them and make the rough places smooth. . . . I will not forsake them" (42:16b).

J. B. Phillips wrote a book called *Your God Is Too Small.* Isaiah did not have that problem. Isaiah served a big God—The Holy One of Israel. Isaiah's "Wonderful Counselor, Mighty God, Everlasting Father, Prince of Peace" (9:6) rules the night as well as the day.

Point of Help

I will select one quality of God and meditate on it today.

Bert's Prayer

The shadows seem to be closing in around me. The job doesn't seem to be too big, but I seem to have become too small. Eternal God, show me the answer. Things have gone wrong somewhere. What am I doing amiss? I will not quit. I will wait for a renewal that only You can bring.

Perspective

I call upon the LORD, who is worthy to be praised, so I shall be saved from my enemies. . . . You gave me a wide place for my steps under me, and my feet did not slip.
                                —Psalm 18:3, 36 NRSV

Point of Hope

When we feel sorry for ourselves, God provides a new perspective.

Are you still attempting to be a patient, kind, loving caregiver on your own strength? You know the look—the synthetic smile, the tone of voice that is a little too even.

One day I had a severe case of cabin fever. I was tired of the routine, dripped dry from the never-ending, tedious food preparation, weary of the constraints of the diabetic lifestyle. In confusion of mind and spirit, I voiced an inward prayer of complaint while outwardly keeping on with the day's duties.

As the hours wore on, words from the Eighteenth Psalm crept into my mind. David wrote this song of praise after he finally gained victory over his enemies. He says that the Lord gave him a wide place. The image is of a narrow mountain path that finally broadens to allow sure footing. Then, David says, he was able to pursue and strike down his opponents (vv. 37–38). As I meditated on the words of the psalm, gradual calm settled over me. The Lord was giving me a wide place for my own steps, spiritual and mental maneuvering room to back away, take aim, and strike down my enemies, self-pity and discouragement. When I got this new perspective, I realized how much I had for which to praise God. As David reminds us, He is our strength, rock, fortress, deliverer, and refuge (vv. 1–2).

Point of Help

When I find myself hemmed in by discouragement, I will ask the Lord to give me a new outlook.

Bert's Prayer

Dear Heavenly Father, renew a right spirit within me, and give me a grateful heart. Teach me to be grateful when I feel oppressed. Let self-pity be replaced by a spirit of gratitude for the things I do have. Keep me continuously aware that I depend upon your power for my existence.

Repair

And the God of all grace, who called you to his eternal glory in Christ, after you have suffered a little while, will himself restore you and make you strong, firm and steadfast.

—1 Peter 5:10

Point of Hope

Jesus mends things.

The word Peter used to describe what God will do for us—a Greek word translated as *restore* or *perfect*—is the same word Matthew used to describe what James and John were doing when Jesus called them to be disciples. They were sitting in the boat mending their nets (Matt. 4:21). They were restoring things that had been damaged by hard use.

After you have been jerked around, soaked repeatedly in cold water, hauled up and down, and asked to carry more than you can bear, what would it be like to have Jesus sit down cross-legged, take you on His lap and mend—restore—you? That is what Peter says our Lord will do for us after we endure the many stresses of the day.

Peter does not say that God will send an angel to do that job. He says that Christ "will himself restore, support, strengthen, and establish you" (1 Pet. 5:10 NRSV).

Dear old Bible commentator Matthew Henry remarks that it was commendable of the boys to mend the old nets rather than ask their father for money to buy new ones. Aren't you glad Jesus never gives up on us but is willing to restore us? He continues to love us, to mend our flaws, to make us useful again after the pressures of the day have taken their toll. The next time you believe you cannot stand one more instance of being slung down on the deck, remember that Jesus mends broken things.

Point of Help

What broken thing in my life can I carry to Jesus today?

Bert's Prayer

My Lord and my God, forgive me for allowing physical pain to become an excuse. Lord, there is still work I can do and that I must do. You have placed me here for a particular purpose. Renew my determination and give me the will to get on with the job. Let my remaining days be offered more in the service of Him whose I am.

Tumult

Brace yourself like a man; I will question you, and you shall answer me.

−Job 38:3

Point of Hope

I know that my Redeemer lives and that I will see Him someday.

The Lord does not always explain Himself. The Lord never told Job that He felt sorry for him. God never explained His dialogue with Satan. Job did not know that God was counting on him to prove to Satan that there were people in the world who were willing to be absolutely faithful. God never explained Job's suffering.

Instead He told Job to brace himself and answer some questions (Job 38:1–3). The vision of God that followed did not come to Job as he sat beside still waters. Instead, the revelation of God's greatness howled in a tempest.

"Where were you when I laid the earth's foundation?" God asked. "Do you know the laws of the heavens?" (Job 38:4, 33). The Lord's persistent questions reduced Job to rubble (Job 42:1–6). Yet a strange comfort permeates Job's response. In a generation that supposed you would die if you ever saw God, Job cries in delight, "Now my eyes have seen you" (Job 42:5). Job comes to the end of himself. This holy hurricane propels him toward God. Assured of God's power, Job is going to make it.

Now and then we caregivers must assess a situation, make a decision, and act upon it in less time than it takes to tell it. In the tumult of such a moment, spiritually speaking, go stand where you can feel the wind of God's Spirit in your face. Look up and see His hawk soaring, the eagle flying high (Job 39:26–27). Let God's strength carry you through the catastrophes of the day.

Point of Help

I will look for evidence of God's creative genius: my own hand, a budding tree, a child.

Bert's Prayer

We are surrounded by the appearance of disaster, but all is not lost. The eternal truths that have seen us through so many storms are still there. For them we give thanks. Loving Father, give us the will to continue the search for that which we have not apprehended and the zeal to continue teaching that which is already ours.

Gratitude

Give us today our daily bread.

—Matthew 6:11

Point of Hope

Caregivers find themselves thankful for things most people do not think about.

Like most Christian families, Bert and I always said the blessing, a short prayer of thanks for the food, before we ate. As with many such prayers, ours had become automatic, prayed without much thought. That changed abruptly one afternoon.

I had been out doing errands. When I got home, I found Bert standing in the kitchen, but "out of it," deep in insulin reaction. He needed food immediately.

Sometimes people in insulin reaction become belligerent and uncooperative. Thankfully, I was able to persuade Bert to sit down and drink a small can of orange juice while I held it. After about twenty minutes, he was able to tell me the last thing he remembered before losing consciousness—he never did remember my arriving home or feeding him.

That experience energized our routine table blessing into one of the most sincere prayers of the day. What if food had not been available when I found him? If necessary, I would have given every cent I had for that little can of orange juice. It saved my husband from serious physical harm.

Caregivers frequently become aware of how much easier our lives are because of the everyday things that most others take for granted—easy access to food, packages of sterile bandages, wheelchair-accessible buildings.

Point of Help

I will count the small items in my kitchen and be grateful for the work they save me.

Bert's Prayer

Loving Lord, let me learn the lesson of affliction. My suffering has already taught me much, and for this I am grateful. But there is more. Your Word is inexhaustible, and so is Your will for my life. Remove from me all anxiety over my own fate. Remind me that my life does have a purpose and that it will not fail.

Hope

Individuals

For what is our hope, our joy, or the crown in which we will glory in the presence of our Lord Jesus when he comes? Is it not you? Indeed, you are our glory and joy.
—1 Thessalonians 2:19–20

Point of Hope

God sees individuals, not a faceless crowd.

Paul says he taught the Thessalonian Christians one by one, as a parent deals with his or her children. The payoff from that individual counseling was huge. Paul says that the children he reared in the Lord will be his hope, joy, and crown (v. 19) when he and his fellow laborers stand before the Lord at Christ's coming.

Do you ever think of the person you care for as evidence that your labor for God has borne fruit? Your crown may consist of one child you taught to live successfully with his or her diabetes. It may be one stroke victim who walked again with your help. It may be one adult whom you fed three times a day for many years.

"Well done, good and faithful servant!" said

the master in Jesus' parable of the talents. "You have been faithful with a few things; I will put you in charge of many things. Come and share your master's happiness!" (Matt. 25:23).

So much of the world's progress involves individual actions. One by one we are born, one by one we learn, eat, work, ail, recover, and finally, die. One by one we will stand before God. Do not be ashamed if you have only one person to present as your hope, joy, and crown.

Point of Help

I will thank God for my ailing loved one, my joy and my crown.

Bert's Prayer

Ah, Lord God, if I can become a channel through which God's message has flowed to a single person, I shall not have lived in vain. Lord, teach me to be a channel of truth, and help me to avoid becoming a hindrance to others.

Relief

The angel of the LORD found Hagar near a spring in the desert; it was the spring that is beside the road to Shur. And he said, "Hagar, servant of Sarai, where have you come from, and where are you going?"

—Genesis 16:7–8

Point of Hope

God has created a plan especially for me.

It had all seemed so simple. Hagar would go home to Egypt and have her baby, surrounded by people who cared about her. Now she was in the wilderness, and the road home had proven longer than she had thought. Hagar had to admit that she was partly to blame for her troubles. If she hadn't said "Nah-nah-nah-nah-nah" in Sarai's face, she could have stayed. Poor little slave girl, she had added poor judgment to her other mistakes.

Then a stranger appeared before her on the wilderness path. El-roi she called Him, the God Who Sees, because He knew all of her past, and it did not matter to Him. He still gave her aid. He had a plan well thought out, created especially for her. Hagar needed only to be obedient to that plan.

From childhood I have known that God loved me. In the midst of caregiving, I wish I had realized how personal that love is, hand tailored just for me. El-roi saw me in the middle of terrifying nights: "for darkness is as light to you" (Ps. 139:12). He saw my torn, grieving heart as I watched Bert suffer. He took into account the tiredness, the mistakes in judgment, my secret rebellions, and He loved me anyway.

Point of Help

I will cast all my anxiety upon God, because He cares for me.

Bert's Prayer

My Lord and the Creator of all things, You could have created us and abandoned us to our fate. You could have, but You didn't. You had plans for us. You call us to the fulfillment of those plans. Let God be thanked. Praise Him for His concern for us. In His care there is peace and contentment. We will offer our thanks daily.

Rescue

The LORD is my rock, my fortress and my deliverer; my God is my rock, in whom I take refuge. He is my shield, and the horn of my salvation, my stronghold.

—Psalm 18:2

Point of Hope

God will do whatever it takes to help us.

In the Eighteenth Psalm, King David describes how he felt when his enemies were threatening his life. They entangled and ensnared him to the point of death (vv. 4, 5). He cried to the Lord for help, and God heard his prayer (v. 6).

What happened next shows the lengths to which the Creator of all the earth will go to help one of His children. David says the earth reeled and rocked on its foundations (v. 7). Smoke, glowing coals, thick darkness, a canopy of clouds, and hailstones were among the weapons launched against the enemy of God's child (vv. 7–12). God mustered all of nature in David's defense.

At the climactic moment, Yahweh Himself appeared. He flew swiftly on the wings of the wind (v. 10), reached down and drew His helpless little one out of deep waters (v. 16).

Why did God put Himself to so much trouble? David says simply that God rescued him "because he delighted in me" (v. 19).

If we believe that God loves all of us equally, can we not take the gorgeous, symbolic language of this psalm as comfort for our own hearts? God is not out there in space somewhere, admiring the stars He created. He is El-roi, the God Who Sees. He is also Emmanuel, God with us, available to deliver me from my own deep waters. All I have to do is ask.

Point of Help

I will ask for God's help, believing that He will give it.

Bert's Prayer

Dear Heavenly Father, I am thankful that my Creator is my friend, One who is interested in me as an individual, and who even has a purpose for my life. When I do anything contrary to Your will, I am hindering that purpose. My sin displeases You. It is marvelous to remember that You are so concerned with my good.

Survival

Show me your ways, O LORD, teach me your paths; guide me in your truth and teach me, for you are God my Savior, and my hope is in you all day long.

—Psalm 25:4–5

Point of Hope

Staying close to God is the surest way to survive the rigors of caregiving.

"Caregiving is hell," Barbara said bluntly. "You see their suffering and cannot do one thing about it." Barbara's mother lived with her and her family for nine years, until her mother's death at age ninety-four. They survived an all-too-familiar litany of unexplained falls, mental confusion, digestive upsets, intractable arthritis, and 911 calls followed by hurry-up-and-wait trips to the emergency room.

Barbara is a member of today's sandwich generation, caught between caring for aging parents and managing teenage children. These caregivers have a familiar set of worries: *I'm exhausted. I can't reason with mother. My children need me too. Will my siblings blame me if mother has a medical disaster? Should I put her in a nursing home? No, I can't face that. O, dear Lord, what shall I do?*

Is the answer too simple? The first thing to do is to learn about God. Notice that the psalmist asks first that God teach him. In that learning process, he realizes again how great God's love for him is. Jesus said, "Take my yoke upon you and learn from me, for I am gentle and humble in heart, and you will find rest for your souls" (Matt. 11:29).

Point of Help

This day I will somehow make time to be with God, because that is where my hope lies.

Bert's Prayer

Give me the sense to bring myself into harmony with Your law and with Your plan for my life, O Lord. You have given me a freedom of choice, and for that freedom I give You thanks. But that freedom is a freedom to reject You. Do not let my effort to do Your will become a rejection. Teach me to choose rightly.

Renewal

Those who hope in the LORD will renew their strength. They will soar on wings like eagles; they will run and not grow weary, they will walk and not be faint.

—Isaiah 40:31

Point of Hope

Blest am I that I have Jesus.

I had reached the end of my rope. But I dared not let go because Bert needed me. I told God about it: "I am so tired. Lord, please help me to stay well. I was never this needed before. What would happen to Bert if I got sick? He cannot even inject his own insulin, much less plan menus and cook. He is so helpless it scares me."

As I struggled with insecurity, I came upon these lines from Johann Sebastian Bach's cantata *Heart and Mouth and Deed and Living.* An unknown poet wrote these words for Bach's music in 1723.

Blest am I that I have Jesus,
Oh, how firmly I hold him,
That he bring my soul refreshment

When I'm ill and filled with grief.
I have Jesus, who doth love me
And himself to me entrusteth;
Ah, I'll hence leave Jesus not,
Even though my heart should break.[1]

Isaiah made the same point when he wrote to God's people, "For I am the LORD, your God, who takes hold of your right hand and says to you, Do not fear; I will help you" (Isa. 41:13). This is only one of God's many assurances that He will make a way for us.

Point of Help

I will offer my hand to God for Him to hold.

Bert's Prayer

The Hope for a dawn of a new day more glorious than anything we have ever known is real. But that hope must not conceal the experience of this present day. It is the day the Lord has made. We must rejoice and be glad in it. Loving Lord, let us perform those duties that are assigned to us here and now.

[1]J. S. Bach, *Hertz und Mund und Tat und Leben*, Cantata BWV 147, Breitkopf and Härtel edition, trans. Harry Jansen, Director of Music Ministry, Trinity Avenue Presbyterian Church, Durham, N.C.

Valleys

There I will give her back her vineyards, and will make the Valley of Achor a door of hope.

—Hosea 2:15

Point of Hope

There is a hidden door where trouble opens into hope.

"Down in the valley, valley so low," wails the Appalachian folk song. Thousands of years earlier, David talked about "the valley of the shadow of death" (Ps. 23:4). Isaiah speaks "of tumult and trampling and terror in the Valley of Vision" (Isa. 22:5). We associate valleys with darkness, discouragement, dead ends.

So it is a surprise when the prophet Hosea calls a valley "a door of hope," especially the valley of Achor. *Achor* means trouble. It was in this valley that Israel experienced a distressing event (Josh. 7:24–26). Yet the prophet says that Achor can turn into a door of hope.

As a caregiver, where is your valley of Achor? Has the valley of Alzheimer's disease prevented all sensible communication with your spouse?

Have strokes or chronic disease destroyed your parents' mobility? Did an accident or a birth defect cheat your child—and you—of a normal life?

Notice that Hosea does not say to cheer up because you will soon be out of the valley. He says here and now, in this valley, you can discover an entrance into hope. That seems unlikely.

But I do not understand the Lord's alchemy. I know only that God can give "a crown of beauty instead of ashes" and "the oil of gladness" to those who mourn (Isa. 61:3). I know that I have walked the hard path of Type 1 diabetes with my husband, and somehow God made it a door in our lives for the blessing of others. I do not understand it, but I walked through it just the same.

Point of Help

I will ask my loving God to help me find the door of hope in this valley.

Bert's Prayer

Dear Heavenly Father, the darkness is so constantly before us that we are tempted to forget the light. But your light is there in all its brilliance if we only lift our sights a bit higher. The darkness will never put out your light. It shines forth its constant invitation to become all You can make us. Give us wisdom to see and strength to accept.

Joy

Sunrise

"Meaningless! Meaningless! . . . Everything is meaningless." What does man gain from all his labor at which he toils under the sun? . . . The sun rises and the sun sets, and hurries back to where it rises.

—Ecclesiastes 1:2–3, 5

Point of Hope

My life is not meaningless when the Lord is my light.

Consider the poor fellow in Ecclesiastes who organized his life without God. Focused on himself, he finds nothing of interest in God's wonderful world. His days are all the same, a tedious grind. The sun rises and the sun sets. How boring.

Contrast him with the psalmist, who puts God first in his life. He sees the same sunrise and finds strength and beauty on all sides: "In the heavens [God] has pitched a tent for the sun, which is like a bridegroom coming forth from his pavilion. . . . It rises at one end of the heavens and makes its circuit to the other" (Ps. 19:4b–6).

David personifies the sun as a strong man,

describing each of his days as filled with joy. The sun's days are all alike, but he does not complain about crossing the same sky in the same direction time after time. He just keeps providing heat and light, the task the Lord ordained for him. We dare not think about what would happen to us if the sun quit doing his job.

In spite of medical advances, the routine for most persons with serious physical problems is as predictable as the sunrise. The psalmist's cure for tedium was to keep his eyes on God, not on himself. My job as a Christian caregiver is to keep my face turned to the Lord, who adds sparkle to life, even in the face of monotony.

Point of Help

Today, I will turn my eyes upon Jesus.

Bert's Prayer

O Lord, my Strength, as I pray that God's eternal will may be done, may it be not a prayer of apathy, but a prayer of confidence; not a prayer of hopelessness, but an affirmative recognition of promise; not a prayer of weakness, but a prayer of strength and power; not a prayer of futility, but a call to action. May Your will be enacted in me.

Revelation

"I have loved you with an everlasting love; I have drawn you with loving-kindness. I will build you up again and you will be rebuilt."

—Jeremiah 31:3–4

Point of Hope

I was important enough for God to hand tailor me, one of a kind.

Nineteenth-century Danish philosopher Søren Kierkegaard says there are no crowds before God. Each of us is destined to stand alone before Him someday, a terrifying thought except for the atoning blood of Christ.

The encouraging side of Kierkegaard's statement is that God loves us so much that He takes time to deal with us as individuals. He created each of us with one-of-a-kind irises, fingerprints, and DNA. And he speaks to each of us by name.

After the rushing wind, splitting mountains, and consuming fire were all gone, the Lord spoke to Elijah in "a sound of sheer silence" (1 Kings 19:12 NRSV). On the other hand, He spoke to

Job from the storm (Job 38:1). Samson's parents thought the mysterious visitor who came to them was an ordinary man until He ascended in the flame from their altar (Judges 13:20–23). When the disciples walking toward Emmaus grasped that it was the risen Christ who gave them broken bread to eat, they forgot their weariness and hunger and ran the seven miles back to Jerusalem to share the news with others (Luke 24:13–35).

When caregiving seems hard and endless, ask God to reveal Himself to you. He may come to you in a whirlwind of activity, in stillness, or in the routine of daily life. It will be His custom-built approach to His unique creation—you.

Point of Help

I will press on, knowing that whatever His method, God's purpose is to make me into His likeness.

Bert's Prayer

Dear Heavenly Father, being truly our Father, the one divine, all-good, and all-perfect Father, You know our needs far better than we know them ourselves. Our prayer is that we may be kept continually aware of Your presence and of Your ability to supply our needs. Give us complete readiness to receive the blessings You are so willing to bestow.

Birthday

"For I know the plans I have for you," declares the LORD, "plans to prosper you and not to harm you, plans to give you hope and a future."

—Jeremiah 29:11

Point of Hope

If nobody but Jesus comes to my birthday party, it will still be fun.

Today is my birthday. Bert used to send me an orchid corsage on my birthday and take me out to dinner. Every year the flower came, and every year I was thrilled all over again. This year, in illness and weakness, he has forgotten what day it is. I will not remind him; it would only make him feel bad. Caregivers cannot afford the luxury of hurt feelings over a person who used to be thoughtful but is now too overwhelmed with illness to remember.

I did tell the Lord it was my birthday though, this morning at my quiet time. Immediately, in that wonderful theater of the mind that the Lord does so well, this little image came into my head: it was Jesus, smiling gently, with a handful of balloons. He said, "Congratulations! You made it another year." He did not have to remind me that it was His strength that made it all possible.

Fanciful? Maybe just a little. But our God has a reputation for attention to the details of the lives of ordinary people. This is the same God who helped the unfortunate prophet when he lost a borrowed ax (2 Kings 6:5–7), the same God who told Peter how to fish tax money out of the lake (Matt. 17:27). I think he remembers my birthday—and yours.

Point of Help

I will celebrate my own life today.

Bert's Prayer

My Heavenly Father, may I have the joy that comes from dedication, the satisfaction that comes from service, and, above all, the peace of a transformed life, which makes everything else possible. Let me live with the Christ of Calvary as well as with the Christ of the Mount of Transfiguration, and give me the good sense to know that the two are one.

Vacation

I went down to the grove of nut trees to look at the new growth in the valley, to see if the vines had budded or the pomegranates were in bloom.

—Song of Songs 6:11

Point of Hope

Joy in caregiving, like fine jewelry, usually comes in a small box.

We went to the regional shopping mall in our state's capital today. It was our summer vacation, one day spent twenty-five miles from home. We had lunch in a cafeteria where Bert had lots of food choices. We walked around the mall, then drove to the local farmers' market and bought a bushel of apples. It was fun, a big day by our standards.

Blessed is the marriage where two people enjoy each other for themselves; the tiniest excuse to be together is enough. The Man and the Woman in the Song of Songs, or Song of Solomon as some Bibles title it, go to the orchard to see if the trees have bloomed. It's not a big deal, but it is enough: they are together. What difference does it make where they are?

Insulin-dependent diabetics have difficulty with America's standard vacation, the long automobile trip. We have taken trips like that, but the uncertainty of when and where to find the next meal and how to get adequate exercise makes such traveling so difficult that it is hardly worth it. Shall I whine because we do not pile into the car and drive hundreds of miles a day? Or shall I choose to be happy in the company of a loved one, kept healthy by sticking to a less ambitious schedule?

Point of Help

Mutual love and respect bring joy to caregiving. I will do my part to cultivate those virtues.

Bert's Prayer

My Lord and my God, as I remember the grace that has been showered upon me, I cannot but offer thanks. On this day I feel especially thankful for the power of choice that has been placed within me. I cannot comprehend this power by which I reach out beyond myself and catch glimpses of the eternal. But I can experience it. I give thanks.

Cooperation

You, O LORD, keep my lamp burning; my God turns my darkness into light. . . . With my God I can scale a wall.

—Psalm 18:28–29

Point of Hope

"The joy of the LORD is your strength" (Neh. 8:10).

The Bible is filled with examples of people who were sure they could be successful using their own resources. People as different as Samson (Judg. 16:20), Saul (1 Sam. 16:14), and Peter (Matt. 26:75) all learned the hard way that this approach does not work. Yet the Bible's unmistakable viewpoint is that in spite of our utter inability to do so, God expects us to live victorious lives.

So what are we supposed to do?

The answer to this dilemma is that God wants people to work with Him. Scripture says that the Lord gives light, but you and I must exert our efforts to scale the wall. Where does the energy come from? The joy of the Lord, says Nehemiah. Bert and

I came to realize that, although God's hand of mercy was leading us, He expected us to do our part, as best we knew how, to maintain Bert's health.

That cooperative venture included learning all we could about diabetes. We read books and asked questions. We learned that the successful management of this incurable disease took daily–hourly–attention.

I learned what to do in emergencies, when Bert could not help himself. Bert faithfully took time to exercise and became expert in observing what foods worked best in his diet. Jesus, the source of joy and light, did for us what we could not do for ourselves, providing quiet inner strength in times of stress, patience in aggravation, and sympathy rather than self-centeredness.

Point of Help

I will rejoice! I'm not alone; God and I are in this together.

Bert's Prayer

Our Lord and Savior, can we give honest thanks for an unwanted disaster that comes upon us? Can we rejoice in suffering? Can we be glad for that which is not good? The answer is, Yes! Suffering is not good. But it is our teacher. We are thankful for the lessons taught through it.

Guidance

The LORD has anointed me . . . to bestow on [those who grieve] a crown of beauty instead of ashes, the oil of gladness instead of mourning, and a garment of praise instead of a spirit of despair.

—Isaiah 61:1, 3

Point of Hope

God is a great guidance counselor.

When Jesus read these words to His childhood friends in the synagogue at Nazareth, folk did not receive Him kindly. In fact, they ran Him out of town (Luke 4:18–30). But Jesus went right on doing the things He had outlined.

The gladness Christ bestows comes when I find the special way He intended for me to spend my life, a calling that is right for me, work that is important in His sight. My first assignment is to find that work, following Him in obedience to that calling. In return, He promises to free me from a life with no meaning—"a spirit of despair" Isaiah calls it.

Messiah's followers need not live in the ashes of our own blunders. He covers our mistakes and

100

sins with His beautiful forgiveness. Knowledge that my sins are cleansed and that I am doing the job God selected for me replaces hopelessness with joy. I did not become a caregiver by accident. Knowing that my work is valuable in God's sight clothes me in Isaiah's "garment of praise" in place of the rags of depression. In Isaiah's day, a happy occasion was fêted by pouring expensive and fragrant oil over one's head, the "oil of gladness." Let today be my day to receive it from Christ's hand.

Point of Help

I will renew my dedication to caregiving because I know that this is the task God has chosen for me right now.

Bert's Prayer

O Lord, the length of one life is so short that its impact on the world is scarcely observable. But from the courts of heaven, You give the good news that Christ gave the ultimate sacrifice, His death, so that every life would have meaning. Heavenly Father, may I give my own life without complaint or remorse.

Love

Tranquility

"Peace I leave with you; my peace I give you. . . . Do not let your hearts be troubled and do not be afraid."

—John 14:27

Point of Hope

God still loves me.

My prayer time this morning was a perfect mess. I felt hurried and pressured. What caregiver does not? I kept mumbling one prayer over and over: "Lord, help Bert understand what the doctor wants him to do and be willing to do it." Finally, it seemed as if the Spirit said, "I heard that. Please move on to something else."

The worst result of muddling up your devotional time is facing the day without the inner satisfaction of having spoken with the Lord at the beginning of the day. I said as much to the Lord in an arrow prayer later in the day, and the Spirit's quiet inner voice spoke the same words Jesus said to another confused woman long ago: "Neither do I condemn you. Go now . . . " (John 8:11).

The reassurance that God still loved me made

up for a lot that went wrong later that day. Christ commands that we not let our hearts be troubled, as if it required an act of our will to still our troubled spirits. Tangled prayers are not sin; it is we who manufacture the shame, with a little help from Satan, always more than ready to accuse us (Rev. 12:10). God refuses to let guilt and confusion define our lives. All we need do is carry our mess to Him, and He will give us back our lives, with hope.

Point of Help

I take comfort in knowing that God loves me even when I am not at my best.

Bert's Prayer

My Lord and my God, I am thankful for having been given another day on earth. I am thankful for my stay here even though I am confident that what lies beyond will be infinitely better. I am thankful because I know that while I am here I have the opportunity of serving You, my Master, in ways You planned. It is a privilege indeed!

Obedience

"The King will reply, 'I tell you the truth, whatever you did for one of the least of these brothers of mine, you did for me.'"

—Matthew 25:40

Point of Hope

Like me, Jesus did not enjoy some parts of His job.

"I did not ask for this job!" my friend cried. "When I married him, he was an athlete. Look at him now!" Disgust tinges her voice. Her husband was diagnosed with multiple sclerosis some time ago. Now the tremors and unsteadiness characteristic of the disease are taking their toll. She must be a caregiver, like it or not.

We read in the Bible of many people who had jobs they did not want. Jesus, who did not want to die but did so, comes first to mind (Luke 22:42). Moses must have been the most reluctant spokesman in history (Exod. 4:10–13). Jonah was so addled by his distaste for the Ninevites that he actually thought he could get away from God's call by taking a ship headed west instead of east (Jon. 1:2–3).

After some personal turmoil, each of these persons did what God asked of him. Why? Did Jesus go to the cross because he wanted to or because it was His Father's will? Was it loyalty to his fellow Hebrews or obedience to God that drove Moses back to Egypt? Jonah's prayer indicates that he went to Nineveh not because he loved the people there but because he had chosen to answer God's call (Jon. 2:2–9).

Caregivers who serve only as a duty to a loved one may find bitterness in the end. The caregiver whose first focus is on rendering service to God will find the yoke easy and the burden light (Matt. 11:28–30).

Point of Help

Today, with God's help, I will look for a new way to turn caregiving into a labor of love.

Bert's Prayer

Dear Heavenly Father, why should I be in this position? Is there a reason for my having this job? I received the job by human means, but it was God who prepared the way. Why? You call me to do a competent job, but there is more. Lord, keep that higher task before me, and forbid that I should fail.

Laughter

*"Where were you when I laid the earth's foundation, . . .
while the morning stars sang together and all the angels
shouted for joy?"*

—Job 38:4, 7

Point of Hope

God created the world with no help from me.

Tonight when I started to pray my usual bedtime prayer, with its long list of family and friends for the Lord to bless, it suddenly became so hum-drum that I couldn't stand it. Surely when the Lord taught us to pray, He must have had in mind more than a routine, "Bless A, B, C, and D."

I saw in my mind's eye a rollicking God (I say it reverently), Creator of happy babies and laughing children, Giver of resilient middle years and serene old age. I saw a God of good humor whose Bible contains puns and records people doing outrageous things, for example, carrying on a conversation with a donkey (Num. 22:28–30).

Abruptly I was taken into the presence of the God who made gray squirrels and crickets, who endows people with a sense of comic timing, who made dogs to love us and cats to disdain us. He gifted each of us with the uniquely human ability to appreciate humorous situations and to laugh at them. It is another way we are made in His image (Gen. 1:26).

My unanticipated vision of the Almighty as a God of mirth was my day's point of help. It transformed my prayer from pious boredom to thanksgiving. "Bless my loved ones" turned into, "Thank you for A, B, C, and D. Thank you for this day. Thank you for being a God of laughter. Thank you for helping me not to take myself too seriously, even in the rigors of caregiving."

Point of Help

I will smile, knowing that the weight of the world is not on my shoulders; it's on God's.

Bert's Prayer

My loving Lord, I want to so live this day that those with whom I chance to speak may feel better because I am here. But I cannot do this—I cannot even start—under my own power. I look to You, the giver of all strength and all authority. Lord, have mercy upon me. Show me the Way.

Duty

*Then the angel of the L*ORD *told [Hagar], "Go back to your mistress and submit to her. . . . You are now with child and you will have a son. You shall name him Ishmael. . . ." So Hagar bore Abram a son, and Abram gave the name Ishmael to the son she had borne.*
—Genesis 16:9, 11, 15

Point of Hope

Love may be spelled d-u-t-y.

What kind of reception do you suppose Hagar received when she walked back into Abram and Sarai's camp? Ordinarily, runaway slaves were dealt with harshly. But this slave was returning to serve a woman she despised, not because she wanted to, but in obedience to God's will. Sarai and Abram must have believed her story. Otherwise, why would Abram have given the child the name that God selected before he was born, Ishmael, which means God hears?

It was Hagar, young, pregnant, scared, miserable, and alone, who called the Man who met her on the wilderness path El-Roi, the God Who

Sees. "You see me!" she said. "You know I'm here! Help me, and I will do my duty!"

Was God's presence so evident in Hagar's face and bearing that Abram could not mistake it? Centuries later, unbelievers looked at Christ's followers Peter and John, saw they were "unschooled, ordinary men" and "were astonished and they took note that these men had been with Jesus" (Acts 4:13).

Caregiving can be monotonous, frightening, and physically and emotionally exhausting. What a difference it makes when you know that El-Roi, the God Who Sees, is standing by in compassion. He is ready to aid His struggling child who is attempting to express love by faithful commitment to the task. You are not alone. He sees and knows and loves you.

Point of Help

How can I reflect God's love in the way I approach others today?

Bert's Prayer

What shall I do, Lord? That question was asked long ago, and I ask it now. But the Way has been made clear. I have heard the message. Give me the will to do that which I know I ought. Forgive my past lethargy, and forbid that I should carry it any more. Increase within me both wisdom and enthusiasm.

Shipping

When I said, "My foot is slipping," your love, O LORD, supported me.

—Psalm 94:18

Point of Hope

God's everyday love is gentle but thorough.

It is God's love that holds us up. We read of being saved by the Lord's strong right arm and of how He fights for His people (Ps. 77:15). But the thing that props us up for the everyday journey is His love.

Did you ever pack a fragile object for shipping? Did you use peanuts, those weightless white plastic chips? The best way to use them is to stand the object in the middle of the box, with some peanuts under it, then pour the peanuts all over and around it. Don't be stingy with your peanuts. Keep pouring until they fill every crevice around even the most irregular shape. These odd little particles are not heavy or suffocating, yet they protect and support.

That is the way God supports us with His love.

He is not grudging with it. And he does not send us out to our assigned tasks with threats or stern admonitions to "just buck up." Instead, He keeps pouring His gentle love over us until it surrounds us, filling every cranny of our lives like divine plastic peanuts, cradling us for shipping through life's bangs and crashes.

Point of Help

Today I will give thanks for places in my life where the Lord's love is supporting me.

Bert's Prayer

I will rise up and hold my head high, for my assignment in this world is from You, the eternal God. You gave me this job; therefore, it must have some purpose. It was by Your hand that I was created, and You have never done a useless thing. Work done in Your name, loving Lord, cannot but be filled with meaning.

Bedrock

And now these three remain: faith, hope and love. But the greatest of these is love.

—1 Corinthians 13:13

Point of Hope

Love underlies successful caregiving.

I was not thinking, or I would never have done such a thing. As Bert and I talked with a group of Bert's law students one day, I addressed Bert as "Sweetie." If my woman's-intuition antennae had been deployed correctly, I would have picked up the waves of suppressed mirth at the thought of Prof. Sparks as "Sweetie." Is she addressing the guy who regularly mauls us in class in order to prepare us for the rigors of practicing law? (Bert was known as a hard teacher. However, he received lots of thank-you letters years later from grateful former students.)

It was misunderstood in that company, but Bert was my Sweetie. A bedrock of love and commitment underlay our lives.

Love is the secret of successful caregiving.

114

"Faults are thick where love is thin," says a Scottish proverb. If we do not love and respect the person who is becoming increasingly helpless before our eyes, the developing disabilities will appear to us as contrariness on the part of the patient. "This person is being ornery and uncooperative just to annoy me," we think. Such judgments readily turn into accusing words and even physical aggression against a person too weak physically or mentally to defend himself.

Where does love for an individual who is no longer the person we knew come from? Surely not from within ourselves. The Holy Spirit Himself plants love, peace, patience, and the other six varieties of His fruit in our lives (Gal. 5:22–23).

Point of Help

I will ask the Lord for more love for the person for whom I care.

Bert's Prayer

Compassionate Lord, again I offer thanks for the ability to render a service for which there is a demand. I will not concern myself with the magnitude of that service. It is enough that it is wanted. Let whatever talent I possess, great or small, be used in the name of Him who gave it.

Patience

Motive

O LORD Almighty, you who examine the righteous and probe the heart and mind, . . . to you I have committed my cause.

—Jeremiah 20:12

Point of Hope

It is not fleeting emotion but steadfast purpose that God honors.

"I lost him at the mall, and my first thought was, 'Yippee! Freedom!' Isn't that awful?"

My friend's husband has Alzheimer's disease. She took him on an outing to the mall to rescue him from the tedium of staring at the same four walls all day. Distracted for a moment, she turned around to find that he had wandered away. Uninvited, the fantasy thought rose, "I'm free!" followed a split second later by a terrifying realization: "How could this have happened? O God, help us."

She found him again. But the gritty taste of guilt for her unbidden reaction to his disappearance lingers.

Clashing emotions are routine for caregivers. Is this wrong? Have we sinned when we wish that this person we are supposed to love, who is the source of so much stress, would just vanish from our lives? Perhaps our prayer should be the same as Jeremiah's. The Lord probes our hearts and minds; He knows what our real motives are. The Lord understands when we caregivers have too much to do, too many decisions to make, too much turmoil in the soul and confusion in the mind. Remember that Paul's description of the dedicated Christian does not center on momentary reactions but on settled resolve: "Count yourselves dead to sin but alive to God in Christ Jesus" (Rom. 6:11).

Point of Help

I am thankful that the Lord understands when I am perfect in motive and faulty in judgment.

Bert's Prayer

The route is dark, but my faith is in the eternal God. He has never withdrawn His guiding hand from those who trust Him, and He will not withdraw it now. As I go forth in that confidence, my Lord and Savior, give me the will to say so. Let me show forth the glory and the wonder of Him to whom I belong.

Sentinel

And the peace of God, which transcends all understanding, will guard your hearts and your minds in Christ Jesus.

—Philippians 4:7

Point of Hope

God does guard duty.

"I just can't stand to see her suffer." I wondered whom this woman was kidding. Numerous little strokes had robbed her mother of the ability to care for herself. The daughter would have contributed money for her mother's care. But don't talk to her about changing wet beds or taking an incapacitated person to doctor appointments. Her elderly mother's problems upset this woman so much that her siblings would have to manage their mother's care without her.

It is easy to say to yourself, "Do your duty, and let the Lord judge her someday for being a slacker," but that doesn't take the sting out of it somehow.

One day as I was considering our family's version of the self-proclaimed sensitive soul, I read

Paul's advice to the Philippians to rejoice in everything, not to worry about anything, and to ask God for things with thanksgiving (Phil. 4:6). I thought this was asking quite a lot in a situation where someone is imposing upon you. Paul adds that "the peace of God . . . will guard your hearts and your minds" (4:7). I discovered that the Greek word translated *guard* is a military term. It means to post a sentinel, to protect with a garrison of soldiers.

Think about that. God's peace is on guard duty, even on bad days, keeping bitterness and anger away from my heart and mind. Now that's real security.

Point of Help

If the peace of Christ is keeping watch over me on the outside, the least I can do is to cultivate a loving attitude on the inside.

Bert's Prayer

Heavenly Father, why am I so discouraged, so let down, so demoralized by things around me? I know that You are God and that in You there can be no defeat. Yet I fear defeat. Help my unbelief. Restore to me the confidence that knows not the word defeat. I will yet serve You, and in You my weakness shall become strength.

Purpose

Hear my prayer, O LORD; listen to my cry for mercy. In the day of my trouble I will call to you, for you will answer me.

—Psalm 86:6–7

Point of Hope

The Lord intends for our troubles to transform us into people who are fully submitted to His will.

How many mothers—those ultimate caregivers—have prayed the psalmist's prayer over a sick child? Remember when Abraham sent Hagar and their son Ishmael away into the wilderness? In despair Hagar sat down and began to sob because Ishmael was dying of thirst. The Lord heard the child's cries and showed Hagar how to save her son's life (Gen. 21:15–19).

But what about the millions of mothers and fathers who have cried to God only to have their child die? Where then is the promise of this psalm? Doesn't God understand how parents hurt?

Yes, our loving Lord does understand; God is

122

a parent too. I believe God was there when another mother, Mary, stood at the foot of the cross and watched in helpless horror as her eldest son died in the agony of crucifixion (John 19:25). How could she have known then the larger purpose Jesus' death served?

It's not a silver lining we are looking for. It is a profound knowledge of God's purposes for our lives. What if my caregiving for someone dear ends in the death of that person? Will I be angry, or will I let God use it to strike another blow at my old, sinful self so that I may become "dead to sin but alive to God in Christ Jesus" (Rom. 6:11)?

Point of Help

Today I will look for signs of God's goodness even though I am faced with what appears to be unanswered prayer.

Bert's Prayer

Everyone can give whatever there is of himself or herself to Your service, Master. No one can do more. No one can afford to do less. My Lord and my God, let me see more clearly the opportunity thus set before me. Give me vision to see the difference between an inability to give much and an unwillingness to give all. Reveal unto me myself.

Comprehension

"For my thoughts are not your thoughts, neither are your ways my ways," declares the LORD.

—Isaiah 55:8

Point of Hope

We can never understand all that God does.

Our friend Dave is dying of cancer. He is in agony. Pat, his wife and chief caregiver, arrives at our Tuesday morning prayer group gaunt after another sleepless night. She wonders why the doctors seem powerless to manage Dave's pain.

"Lord," prays one of our number, "we do not pretend to tell you what is healing." Here is truth, for none of us knows what is best for Dave. Do we pray for Dave's healing? Do we pray for more effective pain management? Do we pray for his release in death? We do not even know why Dave is dying rather than one of us. So we pray, explaining to the Lord that we do not understand and asking for some kind of clarity.

Isaiah records God's promise that His word "will not return to me empty, but will . . . achieve the purpose for which [He] sent it" (Isa. 55:11). Isaiah compares God's Word to rain that waters the earth. For reasons we do not fully fathom, this causes the seed to sprout. It produces grain, the grain is made into bread, and by another incompletely understood process, that bread nourishes our bodies (Isa. 55:10). Nowhere does God promise that we will comprehend all of this, nor do we need to. God provides for us just the same whether we understand His ways or not.

Point of Help

I will trust the Lord even when I do not understand His purpose, and I will turn to Him for comfort.

Bert's Prayer

Though the storm clouds gather and the foundations tremble, I will not be afraid, for my confidence rests in You, the eternal God, and You will not fail. I will yet serve You, and in doing so, I shall gain wisdom to understand the woes that now surround me. When I understand them, I am confident they will appear small indeed.

Refocus

Whatever you do, work at it with all your heart, as working for the Lord, not for men. . . . It is the Lord Christ you are serving.

—Colossians 3:23–24

Point of Hope

Be certain to whom you are speaking before you refuse a job.

B ert became angry and yelled at me one night. This was quite out of character. It happened because he misinterpreted what I said. As his illness progressed, he processed what was said to him slowly and, sometimes, erroneously. He wasn't the only one who became annoyed by it.

Yet if Jesus Christ appeared at my door and asked me to feed Him a meal spoonful by infuriatingly slow spoonful, wouldn't I do it graciously because it was He who had asked? Paul says that, in effect, it is Christ whom we caregivers feed, bathe, and clean up after. It is Jesus to whom we repeat the same direction over and over. Paul was speaking to slaves who were members of the

Colossian church when he made this point.

Peter took the same position. "For it is a credit to you if, being aware of God, you endure pain while suffering unjustly," he said (1 Pet. 2:19 NRSV). The Bible's general instruction is to do everything as if it were an offering to God. This moves the spotlight away from poor me, slaving away on this unending treadmill. It focuses attention instead on the other person and the ways that I can better serve him, since I am doing this as if that person were Christ.

Do you think you can do that in your own strength? Think again. Paul said, "Christ gives me the strength to face anything" (Phil. 4:13 CEV).

Point of Help

I will select one irritating circumstance in my life and offer it to God today.

Bert's Prayer

Dear Heavenly Father, unworthy as we are, we come to You in boldness and in confidence. We come not relying on our own worthiness or our own goodness because we know we don't have it. We come because You have invited us to come. Give us a greater love for You that we may be prepared to go out as willing, enthusiastic, eager workers, ready to perform the task that we and we alone were intended to do.

Resistance

Submit yourselves, then, to God. Resist the devil, and he will flee from you. Come near to God and he will come near to you.

—James 4:7–8

Point of Hope

"The one who is in you is greater than the one who is in the world" (1 John 4:4).

Martha's Prayer

Dear Lord, You know about me. Here I stand weighing three ounces of pot roast on the food scales in my kitchen. I've been standing here weighing food for many years now. And Lord, You know about my missionary friends who roam the world, come across old friends in strange airports, and visit world-famous sights on their way from one demanding, interesting assignment to another.

You know how the evil one comes and says, "Don't you wish you had a life like that?" Your Word says to stand firm against the devil, so I will.

Go away, Satan. I defy your efforts to make me feel sorry for myself.

Lord, Your instruction to resist the devil is sandwiched between two of Your commands: submit to God and come near to God (James 4:7–8). Give me strength to do all three—submit, resist, come near. I will beat back this enemy using the sword of the Spirit, Your Word. "Do not gloat over me, my enemy! Though I have fallen, I will rise" (Mic. 7:8).

I, one lone caregiver in a little kitchen at what seems like the end of the world, draw near to You, knowing You see me and pity and forgive and understand—while I weigh pot roast.

Point of Help

I will draw near to God today.

Bert's Prayer

When I seek comfort, I never find it. But when I abandon the chase and give my whole self to God, by Whom and for Whom I was created, comfort is there. Someone told us long ago that we will remain restless until we find rest in the Creator. My Lord and my God, make me willing to receive that rest, which is rest indeed.

Strength

Endurance

And we pray this in order that you may live a life worthy of the Lord: . . . being strengthened with all power according to his glorious might so that you may have great endurance and patience, and joyfully giving thanks to the Father.

—Colossians 1:10–12

Point of Hope

God offers strength training.

Paul prays that the Colossians might be spiritually strong, having "all the strength that comes from [God's] glorious power" (Col. 1:11 NRSV). The Greek word Paul uses means "to enable." It also means "miraculous power." It is derived from our old Greek friend *dunamis,* from which we get the English word *dynamite.*

Paul goes on to say that he wants this miraculous power to give us "great endurance and patience." Paul means patience with people, patience for the long haul, long-suffering, bearing with folks no matter how unpleasant they may be.

The Apostle is not finished. He adds joy. Commentator William Barclay says that the

Greek word used here suggests a "radiant, sunny-hearted joy" in any circumstance.

Does this include caregiving? Are we caregivers to face day after day in cheerful, hopeful endurance, giving thanks to the Father in calm delight? Is Paul kidding? Doesn't he realize how wearing it is to care for a chronically ill person?

I think Paul did understand, because he coped with his own thorn in the flesh (2 Cor. 12:7). Paul means what he says, and the only explanation can be that God never intended for us to live the Christian life by ourselves. He says over and over in His Word that He will help us. Judging from Paul's carefully chosen words to the Colossians, it will not be sparing help, either.

Point of Help

What exercise can I do today that will strengthen my spiritual muscles?

Bert's Prayer

Our Heavenly Father, as we go into the world, may we be worthy of Him in whose name we go. Keep us aware that we are His ambassadors, sent forth to proclaim the good news of His resurrection. We know we cannot deliver that news unless we have received it. Transform our lives into conformity with our assigned task.

Priority

"Call to me and I will answer you and tell you great and unsearchable things you do not know."
—Jeremiah 33:3

Point of Hope

The first priority of a caregiver is not action but prayer.

Every great revival of Christianity seems to have begun with earnest prayer by a small group of persons. The nineteenth-century Haystack Revival began when a group of college students met twice weekly at a haystack to pray. It turned into a general revival of interest in Christianity in the United States. A youthful Billy Graham prayed with a group of friends one evening at Winona Lake, Indiana, an event some persons count as the birth of Dr. Graham's ministry to millions. Prayer first has always been God's order. The disciples waited in Jerusalem until the Holy Spirit came (Luke 24:49). The rest, as they say, is history (Acts 2).

What has all of that to do with me? Somewhere

amid my daily routines, there must be time for my personal Bible reading and prayer. But how can I pray when I am on this caregiver's treadmill? It is never easy to keep a consistent daily devotional time, even in the best of times. When an incapacitated person's schedule must be considered, it seems impossible. It may mean getting up earlier or going to bed later. It may mean turning off the television. Perhaps it involves some private sacrifice known only to me.

Is it worth the effort? Consider the alternatives: losing touch with God, coming to a crisis or a decision with no scripture fresh in mind, or having no one to cry to when caregiving becomes overwhelming.

Point of Help

I will call out to the Lord in prayer today.

Bert's Prayer

Truly we must be both wise as serpents and harmless as doves. My Lord and my God, teach us the cunning necessary to our own preservation, and remind us that in being preserved we are preserved for service. Prepare us for that service. Make clean our hearts, and give us stronger wills that we may become eager for the task that is set before us.

Communion

Then he climbed into the boat with them, and the wind died down.

—Mark 6:51

Point of Hope

Time alone with Jesus brings calm.

We caregivers think some days will never end. Jesus and the disciples had days like that.

Do you remember the time the crowds pursued Jesus and His disciples until "they did not even have a chance to eat"? It got so bad that Jesus finally said, "Come with me by yourselves to a quiet place and get some rest" (Mark 6:31). The crowds followed them. It got to be suppertime. Jesus multiplied the loaves and fishes, but guess who had to get the folks organized, seated, and served—the disciples (Mark 6:38–44). Then they had to deal with the leftovers. Finally, Jesus pushed His students into the boat with instructions to cross the lake. Jesus dismissed the crowd and at last managed a little time to pray.

In the meantime, things did not work out for the disciples. An adverse wind came up, and it was as if they were rowing against a wall. Then Jesus emerged in the strangest way, walking on the water. Do you recall when it was that the wind went down and they finally got a little rest? It was when Jesus came into the boat with them (Mark 6:51).

The record does not indicate that they spent only peaceful days alone with the Master after that. Oh, no. As soon as they moored the boat, "people recognized Jesus. They ran . . . and carried the sick on mats to wherever they heard he was" (Mark 6:54–55).

The busyness begins again for caregivers every day also. The secret to keeping sanity is to carve out little bits of time in the boat—for communion with Christ.

Point of Help

No matter what, I will shoehorn some time out of this day to spend a quiet moment with Jesus.

Bert's Prayer

My loving Lord, it is easy to allow the visible to crowd the invisible from my thoughts. The more that happens, the more my thinking becomes disordered and confused. Then I remember that everything that is "me" was created to work only one way. You are that Way. Keep me in it.

Courage

Give me a sign of your goodness, that my enemies may see it and be put to shame, for you, O LORD, have helped me and comforted me.

—Psalm 86:17

Point of Hope

What I cannot stand, God can.

"I'd like to think I'm not envious," Sarah told me, but she obviously was. "We see families doing this and that together, and we are left in the dust. We can't go to the beach, you know, because sand and wheelchairs don't mix. I would not wish this walk on anyone." Sarah's eleven-year-old son, Mark, was born with a brain tumor. He had a stroke during surgery to remove it. As a result, his sight and hearing are limited, and he must spend most of his time in a wheelchair.

"It seems as if people are just waiting for us to crack up." Sarah begins to cry. "Without the Lord in my life, I couldn't take it. Our marriage would be in trouble. I don't know what I'd do."

Have you been there?

Sarah's bout of self-pity was short lived. She continued, "It isn't the be-all and end-all if we don't have a wonderful life. All through the Bible people suffered: some were healed; some weren't. God can work what we go through for good, accomplishing what He wants. We have to embrace it. I try to think of the impact Mark's life has made on others."

Sarah and her husband join most loving caregivers when they acknowledge that the selfless love needed to keep on comes only from God. This is caregiving at its best.

Point of Help

I will remember that it's not a wonderful life but a heavenly perspective that matters most.

Bert's Prayer

Sympathetic Christ, may I never be kept from my post of duty by any desire for personal comfort or individual safety. Let my eyes be opened wide that I may see clearly the road to duty, and let my will be so firm that I have no question of whether or not to follow that road.

Assignment

Bring joy to your servant, for to you, O Lord, I lift up my soul.

—Psalm 86:4

Point of Hope

God can make something interesting out of monotony.

Tedium is the caregiver's middle name. Managing almost any chronic disease involves endless routines. In my case it was coming up with the proper diabetic diet three times a day, 365 days a year. In some ways it was easy to do because the menu had to be simple—things like plain broiled meat with boiled or baked vegetables. Casseroles and fancy sauces made it too difficult to calculate the calories.

But as the lady said, life is so . . . *daily*. No matter how tired we were or how inconvenient it was, Bert still had to follow his diet plan. The food had to be on time, too, because diabetics who inject insulin must eat on a strict schedule if they are to stay fit. I couldn't blame Bert; he was not picky. It was the disease that forced the constraints upon us. By the time I got everything cooked and his portions measured, frankly, sometimes I wanted to throw the plate against the wall. I never did. Yet I wanted to.

Then it was time to pray with the psalmist, "In the day of my trouble I will call to you, for you will answer me" (Ps. 86:7). Notice that the psalmist's prayer is predicated upon honest devotion to his God. He refers to himself as God's "servant who trusts in you" (v. 2). Now that is "praying ground."

Point of Help

I will commit the tedium of my job to the Lord.

Bert's Prayer

I am grateful, O Lord, for the assignment given me this day and for the gift of courage to perform it. Actually, it was a little thing. But never before in my life have I been so conscious of a specific order from You. Since it was Your act, not mine, may I never take any personal pride in its performance or credit for the results.

Growth

Now the LORD God had formed out of the ground all the beasts of the field and all the birds of the air. He brought them to the man to see what he would name them; and whatever the man called each living creature, that was its name.

—Genesis 2:19

Point of Hope

Learning new things is a way of growing.

God let Adam name the animals. It would have been faster and easier for God to name them Himself. He made them; He surely understood them. But He let Adam struggle with it. Why?

Think of how much better Adam must have understood his fellow creatures after laboring with this project. He must have strained and squirmed to get them into the proper categories. Cats, horses, and goats all have four legs, but there was more to it than that. Adam had to devise a system for describing their differences, not just settle for the ways in which they were the same. Did all the fish look alike at first? But the more Adam studied them, the more differences he must have observed. Surely he grew intellectually because of this exercise.

When God first approached Adam with the job, do you think Adam saw it as an opportunity for mental development? I doubt it.

It is a truism that the more you know about a disease, the better you can manage it. So we care-givers learn for the good of the victim. But learn for yourself too. No matter how much you resent the intrusion of chronic illness or the aftermath of an accident upon your life, don't let this cruel malady win. Turn it into a path to intellectual growth. Unexpected consequences may surface. You may wind up with new friends; you may help others; they may help you.

Point of Help

I will increase my knowledge of this infirmity as a way of doing something good for myself.

Bert's Prayer

Our Lord and our God, let us not be afraid of that which lies beyond our present understanding, but let us look upon it as a challenge and an opportunity. Let it stand as a sure testimony that we may still grow, that our horizons may yet be extended. He who gave us our sense of awe and wonder will also see to its fulfillment.

Wisdom

Relief

*Should I not be concerned about [Nineveh] that great
city?*

—Jonah 4:11

Point of Hope

Sometimes the Lord says, "Lighten up."

When we got home from the doctor's office, I was
angry. Our questions were either unanswered or
treated with what I thought was contempt.

A version of the Lord's question to Jonah
crept into my mind. "Do you do right to be angry
with a person over whom you have no control?"
I made a version of Jonah's reply, "Yes, I am jus-
tified in being angry" (Jon. 4:4, 9).

The prophet Jonah may be the only evangelist
in history who fumed because people responded
to his preaching. You recall that he did not want
to answer God's call to preach in Nineveh, but he
went reluctantly after his experience with the
great fish (1:17). To his disgust, the Ninevites
repented. Jonah went outside the city and sat
down to watch, evidently hoping God would

destroy the place (4:5). Instead, God caused a vine to come up to give Jonah shade. Then the plant died, and Jonah got mad about that too. The Lord pointed out to him that the bush, its life and death, were not under Jonah's control, implying that it was hardly important anyway. What did matter were the people of Nineveh and even their animals (4:11).

"What are you saying to me, Lord?" I prayed. That I should not take myself so seriously? That this doctor is not under my control, and there is no sense in wasting energy being angry with him? That God loves the doctor as much as He loves me?

Yes, Martha, all of the above.

Point of Help

With God's help, I will take today's crisis and myself less seriously.

Bert's Prayer

Dear Heavenly Father, even when we think we are honestly trying to serve as ambassadors of the eternal God, we find it hard to do it Your way. The way of the still, small voice seems ineffective compared with the blare of publicity that we are well equipped to use. Search our hearts. Let our ego be submerged in Your service.

Planning

The plans of the diligent lead to profit as surely as haste leads to poverty.

—Proverbs 21:5

Point of Hope

God is our helper, but He expects us to make sensible plans.

While driving with friends one day, I made a quick stop in traffic. The jolt sent a small can of orange juice rolling out from under the car seat. One of the women picked it up and handed it to me. "Did you know this was under the seat?" she asked.

Yes, I knew it was under the seat. What I did not tell her was that two more cans had probably broken their moorings and were rolling around somewhere too.

Diabetics who inject insulin live a hand-to-mouth existence nutritionally. At every meal they must carefully balance food intake against insulin dose in a strict time frame. To inject insulin without being certain where your next meal is coming from is courting disaster.

The orange juice in the car was insurance that if Bert should be delayed in traffic, food would be available if needed. Along with his billfold and his keys, two or three lumps of sugar were among the items always carried in his pockets. A banana fit handily into the inside breast pocket of his jacket. He might not need it, but it was there just the same, bringing peace of mind. If an unexpected event postponed a meal, he was equipped to head off insulin reaction before it overcame him. He had planned ahead. He was ready for whatever the day brought.

Point of Help

I will help my infirm loved one create practical strategies to cope with the unexpected.

Bert's Prayer

Why should I fear? God, You placed me here and gave me this assignment. You are able to perform that which You undertake. I will rejoice, not in my suffering or even in my hope for what is yet to come, but in my privilege of serving the Eternal here and now. My weakness is Your strength. I will be glad.

Sweetener

And I will put my Spirit in you and move you to fol-
low my decrees and be careful to keep my laws.
—Ezekiel 36:27

Point of Hope

Every place is hallowed ground when God's
Holy Spirit dwells within us.

The ancient priests of Israel met with God's Holy
Spirit before the mercy seat, whose lid supported two solid gold cherubim which knelt facing each other, their wings covering the top of the
covenant box (Exod. 37:6–9).

Ezekiel's prophecy looked down the centuries
to a time when God's Spirit would reveal Himself
not just at the mercy seat on specified occasions,
but within believers at all times. Jesus instructed
the disciples to expect this event. You will know
Him, Christ said, "for he lives with you and will
be in you" (John 14:17).

This is what the eighteenth-century English
poet William Cowper had in mind when he wrote:

Jesus, where'er thy people meet,

There they behold thy mercy seat;
Where'er they seek thee thou art found,
And every place is hallowed ground. . . .
Here may we prove the power of prayer
To strengthen faith and sweeten care.

Our God is a God of the local; He meets us where we are. Holy living was meant to be a practical, here-and-now lifestyle, not an ethereal, otherworldly one. Our relationship with the Holy Spirit is not just vertical. It should reach horizontally to everyone around us.

Point of Help

If the one I care for is unable to pray, I will pray on his or her behalf so that the Holy Spirit may comfort his or her heart as well.

Bert's Prayer

Loving Lord, why should I be discouraged or cast down? My past mistakes rise up to haunt me at every step of the way. Events outside my control block my every move. But over and above it all rings the voice of Him who said He would be with me always, even to the end of the world. He is my Redeemer.

Instruction

Instruct a wise man and he will be wiser still; teach a righteous man and he will add to his learning.
—Proverbs 9:9

Point of Hope

When that chronically ill person you love says, "This treatment is wrong," he or she may be right.

For thirty-six years Bert set his own insulin doses and decided on the amount and timing of his meals. But as Bert grew older and unrelated health problems developed, I took over the insulin injections according to a new doctor's management system. "This new system you and the doctor thought up is killing me!" Bert lamented.

I was caught between Bert and the doctor. Bert believed I was siding with the doctor against him and felt deserted. The doctor blamed me for not getting Bert into full compliance with what the physician wanted, giving no credit at all to Bert's thirty-six years of successfully managing his own disease.

Bert's system was old-fashioned, but if it worked, why change? This doctor's treatment plan was newer, but was it better?

As I look back over the old records, I realize that many times Bert was right and the doctor and I were wrong. That has become another of those aching *what ifs* and *if onlys* that plague any thoughtful caregiver.

A wise nurse said to me one day, "Pay attention to your body, and do what it says." How I wish I had paid more attention in those days to what Bert's body was telling him.

Point of Help

I will listen to my loved one and take his or her wishes into account when making decisions.

Bert's Prayer

They needed my help. They even asked for it. I failed to give it. I have failed.

O God, forgive me. I might have saved them if I had only tried. I ask to be forgiven, but I also ask for a more resolute heart. For me to gain the peace and contentment that comes from being forgiven is not important. That I may give myself fully when the next opportunity arises is what matters. Lord, make me ready.

Diplomacy

*The LORD delights in the way of the man whose steps he
has made firm; though he stumble, he will not fall, for
the LORD upholds him with his hand.*

—Psalm 37:23–24

Point of Hope

Diplomatic skill, like everything else, comes
from God.

The telephone call was from a friend inviting us
to dinner. "Can Bert eat chicken?" she asked. "I
thought I'd just have a chicken casserole," the
hostess continued. "Can he eat rice?"

I knew it was time to send up an arrow prayer
for the gift of tact.

"Yes," I replied, "he can eat both chicken and
rice, but how much of each he gets and when he
eats are important."

Such conversations always frustrated me. I
feared the attempt to ward off a fiasco made me
sound unappreciative. We did not want to
become hermits, never accepting invitations, but
dinner in the home of friends could be difficult.

People meant well, but most did not have any idea what a diabetic's regimen involves. That it is necessary for the insulin-injecting diabetic to eat the same quantity of food at about the same time each day seems unusual, almost unbelievable.

The Bible has much to say about the necessity for wisdom. The Thirty-seventh Psalm has several promises tailored for those of us who sometimes put our feet in our mouths. The psalm says that the righteous person speaks wisdom (v. 30), that our salvation is from the Lord (v. 39), and that the Lord helps and delivers us (v. 40). If I am God's child, then I can claim these promises for tact in dealing with the well-meaning, honest ignorance of others.

Point of Help

I will depend on the Lord for wisdom when responding to others about the rigors of caregiving.

Bert's Prayer

Lord, my frequent prayer is for the removal of pain, but it is not removed. Loving Father, keep me from bitterness, and teach me to bear the pain more graciously. If there is a lesson I am to learn from it, guide me to that lesson. And may I never add to the unhappiness of others by reminding them how I am less fortunate than they.

Honesty

Hear my cry, O God; . . . lead me to the rock that is higher than I.

—Psalm 61:1–2

Point of Hope

"The fear of the LORD is the beginning of wisdom" (Ps. 111:10).

Mother stood in the hall outside her bedroom, her blind eyes turned toward the sound of my voice. "There is something the matter with my mind," she said. "I wish you would tell me what it is."

How do you tell someone who graduated second in her college class that she is failing mentally? Can you tactfully explain that the oxygen is no longer getting to her brain and she is becoming senile?

Mother and I always had an open, honest relationship. Can I give her cruel news now? A gloom different from any emotion I had ever felt settled over me. Mother's misery—and mine—seemed likely to go on as far as the eye could see.

I had to say something, so I suggested that we

go into the family room and I would read to her our evening chapter from the Bible, just as she used to do for me before I was old enough to read. The roles had reversed, and like any toddler, her attention span was so short that she was satisfied with my non-answer. But I wasn't.

Later that night I prayed—again—for God's wisdom. Unforeseen caregiving decisions seemed to whack me in the head constantly. I am so grateful that asking for God's wisdom is not like placing a call on a cellular telephone, the time limited to a few, expensive minutes. I can ask again and again in full assurance that "those who hope in the LORD will renew their strength" (Isa. 40:31).

Point of Help

I will not be shy in seeking wisdom, for God has promised to give it.

Bert's Prayer

I am praying for wisdom again, Lord. Too often I have been unresponsive when You have stood ready to teach me. Loving God, forgive my neglect. Be patient with Your unworthy servant. Extend to me another opportunity. Renew a right spirit within me, and give me the will to do Your will. Use me, Lord, even in my weakness.